(104)	A Bird, (Fisher 1. *Avis,* (here the Kings (hic *Halcyon,* 1. making her nost in mari in the Sea) nidulans,)
150	CL (150)	Actionibus suis præfigit *Scopum* ." Text shown as printed. The first Latin line corresponds to the last English line.
—	CLI (151)	**Chapter CXII** "*Revellers* . babble; *Heluones* . rixantur." The 1659 edition has "brabble", meaning "quarrel" or "brawl". **Chapter CXXVII** *Illustration shown as printed.* For comparison, here is the equivalent illustration from the 1659 edition:

66 • The Orbis Pictus • Comenius, Johann Amos

149	God's Providence	191
110	Prudence	137
	R.	
135	Races	171
23	Ravenous Birds	29
144	Religion	183
34	River-fish	41
82	The Roper	99
138	*Regal* Majesty	174
	S.	
98	A School	119
142	The Sea-fight	180
35	Sea-fish and Shell-fish	42
42	The outward and inward Senses	52
31	Serpents	37
91	Shipwreck	111
200 63	The Shoe-maker	78
18	Shrubs	23
21	Singing Birds	27
131	Sleights	167
118	The Society betwixt Man and Wife	148
120	The Society betwixt Parents and Children	152
121	The Society betwixt Master and Servant	153
43	The Soul of Man	54
139	The Souldier	176
69	The Black-smith	85
136	Boys Sports	172
104	The Celestial Sphere	127
107	The Terrestial Sphere	132
100	Arts belonging to Speech	121
77	The Stable	94
130	A Stage-play	166
12	Stones	16
73	The Stove with the Bed-room	89
99	The Study	120
88	Swimming	107
	T.	
62	The Taylor	77
112	Temperance	140
133	Tennis play	169
107	The Terrestial Sphere	132

125	The Torments of Malefactors	159
83	The Travellor	100
13	A Tree	17
70	The Turner	86
	U.	
25	Flying Vermin	31
32	Crawling Vermin	38
56	The Vintage	70
	W.	
7	The Water	11
60	Weaving	75
74	Wells	90
29	Wild Cattle	35
30	Wild Beasts	36
3	The World	6
92	Writing	112

Trinuni Deo Gloria.

FINIS.

Original Title Page

Joh. Amos Comenii

Orbis Sensualium Pictus:

HOC EST

Omnium principalium in Mundo Rerum, & in Vita Actionum,

Pictura & Nomenclatura.

Joh. Amos Comenius's

VISIBLE WORLD:

OR, A

Nomenclature, and Pictures

OF ALL THE

Chief Things that are in the World, and
of Mens Employments therein;

In above 150 Copper Cuts.

WRITTEN

By the Author in Latin and High Dutch, being
one of his last Essays ; and the most suitable to
Childrens Capacity of any he hath hitherto made.

Translated into E

By Charles Hoo

For the Use of Yo

The Eleventh Edi
the English made
answer Word for

Nihil est in inte
prius fuit in sen

London; Printe
John and *Benj.*
Sprint, at the *B*
1728.

Additional Notes

Editor's Preface:

The text for th
is from the Engli
which for the fi
words were so ar
posite their Latin

The 1659 Engl
same general lay
within sentences
explained in the "
1727 edition.

Chapter Number

In the 1659 edit
Clausula (Close)
in the 1727 editio
ters CIV (104). I
in the numbers v
some illustrations
through 104 were
63–103).

Chapter Name	1 to
Invitation	—
God	I
Shoemaker	L ((
Carpenter	L ((
Geometry	C (
Celestial Sphere	C (
Aspects of the	C

	36	134	Dice-play	170	53	Hunting	66
of a City	181	111	Diligence	139	46	Husbandry	58
	24	45	The Dressing of Gardens	56		I.	
in the ...ods	28		E.		1	The Invitation	1
...s	29	9	The Earth	13	101	Musical *Instruments*	123
	27	106	The Eclipses	131	146	Judaism	186
...nd Bones	50	66	Engines	81	124	Judgment	157
	118	108	Europe	134	150	The last Judgment	193
...der	117		F.		116	Justice	145
...ers Shop	116	58	A Feast	72		K.	
...r	86	132	The Fencing-School	168	137	The Kingdom and Region	173
	172	5	Fire	8		L.	
	63	51	Fishing	64	28	Labouring Beasts	34
	71	34	River-fish and Pond-fish	41	117	Liberality	147
	165				19	Living Creatures	24
	67	35	Sea-fish and Shell-fish	43	59	The dressing of Line	74
		40	The Flesh and Bowels	49	61	Linen Cloaths	76
Sphere	127	15	Flowers	20	80	Looking-glasses	97
	177	25	Flying Vermin	31		M.	
	103	113	Fortitude	141	148	Mahometism	190
...d fro	105	26	Four footed Beasts about the House	32	138	Kingly Majesty	174
	79				36	Man	43
	33	52	Fowling	65	37	The Seven Ages of Man	44
	35	20	Tame-Fowl	25	38	The outward parts of a Man	45
...nd Bones	50	24	Water-Fowl	30			
	187	10	The Fruits of the Earth	14	65	The Mason	80
	154	14	Fruits of Trees	18	127	Measures and Weights	162
of a City	181		G.		126	Merchandizing	161
...rts of a	156	89	A Galley	108	90	A Merchant Ship	109
		145	Gentilism	184	11	Metals	15
	194	103	Geometry	126	68	A Mine	84
	12	2	God	5	105	The Apparitions of the Moon	137
...nsan-	150	149	God's Providence	191			
		47	Grasing	59	109	Moral Philosophy	136
	68	49	Grinding	62	101	Musical Inst'ments	123
	98		H.			P.	
...ier	99	39	The Head and the Hands	47	93	Paper	113
	22				87	Passage over Waters	106
...in	38	16	Pot-herbs	21	114	Patience	142
live as	40	199	Herd-Cattle	33	102	Philosophy	125
...as by		27			109	Moral Philosophy	136
		4	Heaven	7	128	Physick	163
...s	37	48	The making of Honey	61	79	The Picture	96
		84	The Horseman	102	34	Pond-fish	41
...mon-	55	67	A House	82	16	Pot-herbs	21
		72	The parts of a House	88	71	The Potter	87
	95	115	Humanity	144	94	Printing	114

103	Geometria	126	91	Naufragium	111	80	Specularia	
	H.		89	Navis actuaria	108	104	Sphæra co	
36	Homo	43	90	Navis oneraria	109	107	Sphæra ter	
78	Horologia	95	8	Nubes	12	125	Supplicia	
45	Hortorum cultura	56		O.		63	Sator	
115	Humanitas	144	143	Obsidium Urbis	181		T.	
73	Hypocaustum cum Dormitorio	89	16	Olera	21	112	Temperan	
			21	Oscines	27	9	Terra	
	I.			P.		10	Terræ fœt	
5	Ignis	8	132	Palæstra	168	60	Textura	
32	Insecta repentia	38	50	Panificium	63	76	Torstrina	
25	Insecta volantia	31	93	Papyrus	113	59	Tractio Li	
101	Instrumenta Musica	123	72	Partes Domus	88	87	Transitus	
123	Interiora Urbis	156	114	Patientia	142	94	Typograph	
1	Invitatio	1	27	Pecora	33		V.	
146	Judaismus	186	47	Pecuaria	59	86	Vectura	
124	Judicium	157	105	Phases Lunæ	130	85	Vehicula	
150	Jud'm extremum	193	102	Philosophia	125	53	Venatus	
28	Jumenta	34	79	Pictura	96	83	Victor	
116	Justitia	145	51	Piscatio	64	81	Victor	
196	L.		34	Pisces Fluviatiles	41	56	Vindemia	
12	Lapides	15	104	Planet. Aspectus	129	122	Urbs	
54	Lanionia	67	131	Præstigæ	167		Z.	
97	Liber	118	149	Providentia Dei	191	57	Zyhopœia	

An Index of the T

See note on chapter numbers for *T The Close* (151) w references 64–10 (printed as 63–1 silently corrected. ditional errors are Minor differences enization are not n

117	Liberalitas	147	110	Prudentia	137			
61	Lintea	76	142	Pugna Navalis	180			
134	Ludus Aleæ	170	74	Putei	90			
136	Ludi pueriles	172		Q.				
133	Ludus Pilæ	169	26	Quadrupedia & *primum* Domestica	32			
130	Ludus Scenicus	166						
	M.			R.		Chap.	A.	
66	Machinæ	81	138	Regia Majestas	174	37	The Seven	
148	Mahometismus	190	137	Regnum & Regio	173	6	The Air	
35	Marinæ Pisces & Conchæ	42	144	Religio	183	33	Amphibion	
			82	Restio & Lorarius	99	105	The Appar Moon	
48	Mellificium	61		S.				
38	Membra Hominis Externa	45	62	Sartor	77	141	The Army	
			98	Schola	119	100	Arts belon Speech	
127	Mensuræ & Pondera	162	70	Scriniarius & Tornator	86			
126	Mercatura	161	111	Sedulitas	139			
68	Metallifodina	84	42	Sensus externi & interni	52	104	The Aspec Planets	
11	Metalla	15	37	Septum Ætat. Hominis	44			
139	Miles	176	129	Sepultura	165			
49	Molitura	62	31	Serpentes & Reptilia	37		B.	
3	Mundus	6	197	Societas Conjugalis	144	75	The Bath	
99	Museum	120	118			76	The Barbe	
	N.		121	Societas Herilis	153			
88	Natatus	107	120	Soc'tas Parentalis	152	28	Labouring	

Nam *dies novissima*
veniet,
quæ resuscitabit
Mortuos, 2.
voce *Tubæ*, 1.
& citabit *Vivos*,
cum illis
ad *Tribunal*
Jesu Christi, 3.
(apparentis in
Nubibus)
ad reddendam rationem
omnium actorum.

Ubi *pii (justi)* &
Electi, 4.
introibunt in vitam æternam,
in locum Beatitudinis
& novum *Hierosolymam*, 5.
Impii vero,
& *damnati*, 6.
cum *Cacodæmonibus*, 7.
in *Gehennum*, 8.
detrudentur,
ibi cruciandi
æternum.

a vidisti
ummatim res
mnes
uæ poterunt ostendi,
didicisti

the *chief Words*	*Voces primarias*
of the *English* and	*Anglicæ* & *Latinæ*
Latin	*Linguæ.*
Tongue.	
Go on now and	Perge nunc & lege
read	diligenter alias
other good *Books*	bonos *Libros*,
diligently,	ut fias
and thou shalt become	*doctus, sapiens,* &
learned, wise, and	*pius.*
godly.	
Remember these	Memento horum;
things;	Deum time, & invoca eum,
fear God, and call	voca eum,
upon him,	ut largiatur
that he may bestow	tibi
upon thee	*Spiritum Sapientiæ.*
the *Spirit of Wisdom.*	
Farewell.	Vale.

Index
195

Index Titulorum.

See note on chapter numbering. The chapter number for *Invitatio* (1) was missing; there is no entry for *Clausula* (151). Chapter references 64–104 were off by one (printed as 63–103) and have been silently corrected. Only those with additional errors are individually marked.

Cap.	A.	Pag.
141	Acies & <u>Prælium</u>	178
6	Aer	10
46	Agricultura	58
33	Amphibia	40
43	Animi hominis	54
19	Animalia & *primum* Aves	24
7	Aqua	12
13	Arbor	17
119	Arbor Consanguinitatis	150
128	Ars Medica	163
92	Ars Scriptoria	112
100	Artes Sermonis	121
52	Aucupium	65
24	Aves Aquaticæ	30
22	Aves Campestres & Sylvestres	28
20	Aves Domesticæ	25
23	Aves Rapaces	29
	B.	
75	Balneum	91
96	<u>Bibliopegus</u>	117
95	Bibliopolium	116
	C.	
41	Canales & Ossa	50
39	Caput & Manus	47
40	Caro & Viscera	49
140	Castra	177
147	Christianismus	187
4	Cœlum	7
<u>58</u>	Convivium	72
55	Coquinaria	68
135	Cursus Certamina	171
	D.	
44	Deformes & Monstrosi	55
2	Deus	5
<u>67</u>	Domus	82
	E.	
106	Eclipses	131
84	Eques	102
77	Equile	194
109	Ethica	36
108	Europa	134
	F.	
69	Faber Ferrarius	85
64	Faber lignarius	79
65	Faber murarius	80
30	Feræ Bestiæ	36
29	Feræ Pecudes	35
71	Figulus	87
15	Flores	20
113	Fortitudo	141
14	Fructus Arborum	18
17	Fruges	22
18	Frutices	23
	G.	
145	Gentilismus	184

and them,
(being filled with his power)
into the World
to preach of him;
being henceforth to come again
to the *last Judgment*,
sitting in the mean time
190 at the *right hand*
of the Father,
and interceding for us.
From this *Christ* we are called *Christians*,
and are saved in him alone.

(hac virtute impletos)
in Mundum prædicaturos;
olim rediturus
ad *Judicium extremum*,
interea sedens
ad *dextram Patris*,
& intercedens pro nobis.

Ab hoc *Christo* dicimur *Christiani*,
inque eo solo salvamur.

CXLVIII.

Mahometism.

Mahometismus.

Mahomet, 1.
a warlike Man,
invented to himself
a new Religion,
mixed with *Judaism*,
Christianity and *Gentilism*,
by the advice of a *Jew*, 2.
and an *Arian Monk*, 3.
named *Sergius*;
feigning,
whilst he had the *Fit of*
the Falling-sickness,
that the *Archangel*

Mahomet, 1.
Homo bellator,
excogitabat sibi novam Religionem,
mixtam ex *Judaismo*,
Christianismo & *Gentilismo*,
consilio *Judæi*, 2.
& *Monachi Ariani*, 3.
nomine *Sergii*;
fingens,
dum laboraret *Epilepsia*,
Archangelum *Gabrielem*,
& *Spiritum Sanctum*,

Gabriel
and the *Holy Ghost*,
talked with him,
191 using a *Pigeon*, 4.
to fetch Meat out of his Ear.

His *Followers* refrain themselves from *Wine*;
are circumcised,
have many *Wives*;
build *Chapels*, 5.
from the *Steeples* whereof,
they are called to Holy Service
not by *Bells*,
but by a *Priest*, 6.
they wash themselves often, 7.
they deny the *Holy Trinity*:
they *honour Christ*,
not as the *Son of God*,
but as a great *Prophet*,
yet less than *Mahomet*;
they call their *Law*,
the *Alchoran*.

CXLIX.

Gods Providence.

Providentia Dei.

Mens States
192 are not to be attributed
to *Fortune* or

secum colloqui,
adsuefaciens *Columbam*, 4.
petere Escam ex Aure sua.

Asseclæ ejus abstinent se
à *Vino*;
circumciduntur,
sunt *Polygami*;
exstruunt *Sacella*, 5.
de quorum *Turriculis*,
convocantur ad sacra
non a *Campanis*,
sed a *Sacerdote*, 6.
sæpius se abluunt, 7.
negant *SS. Trinitatem*:
Christum honorant,
non ut *Dei Filium*,
sed ut magnum *Prophetam*,
minorem tamen *Mahomete*;
Legem suam vocant *Alcoran*.

Humanæ Sortes non tribuendæ sunt
Fortunæ aut *Ca-*

Chance,
or the *Influence of the Stars*,
(*Comets*, 1. indeed
are wont to portend no good)
but to the provident
Eye of God, 2.
and to his *governing Hand*, 3.
even our *Sights*,
or *Oversights*,
or even our *Faults*.
God hath his *Ministers*
and *Angels*, 4.
who accompany Man, 5.
from his birth,
as *Guardians*,
against wicked *Spirits*,
or the *Devil*, 6.
who every minute layeth wait for him,
to tempt and vex him.
Wo to the mad *Wizzards* and *Witches*
who give themselves
to the *Devil*.
(being inclosed in a *Circle*, 7.
calling upon him with *Charms*)
they dally with him,
and fall from God!
for they shall receive their reward with him.
193

CL.

The Last Judgm

Judicium extren

æneum Serpen- tem, 12. erigi contra morsum Serpen- tum in Deserto. Quæ omnia Typi erant Mes- siæ venturi, quem Judæi adhuc ex- pectant. nigenitus æter- us Dei Filius, 3. romissus rotoplastis in aradiso, ndem conceptus er Sanctum Spir- um sanctissimo tero irginis Mariæ, 1. domo regiâ avidis, indutus hu- anâ carne, rodiit in undum ethlehemæ idæâ, summâ pauper- te abuli, 2. pleto tempore, nno Mundi 970, d mundus ab nni peccato nomen Jesu	world 3970, but pure from all sin, and the name of Jesus was given him, which signifieth a Saviour. When he was sprinkled with *holy Bap- tism*, 4. (the *Sacrament* of the *new Covenant*) by *John* his Forerunner, 5. in *Jordan*, the most sacred *Mystery* of the divine *Trin- ity*, appear'd by the *Father's* voice, 6. (whereby he testi- fied that this was his *Son*) and the *Holy Ghost* in the shape of a *Dove*, 7. coming down from Heaven. From that time, being the 30th year of his Age, unto the fourth year, he declared who he was, his words and works manifesting his Divinity, being neither owned, nor entertained by the *Jews*, because of his voluntary poverty. 189 He was at last taken by these (when he

impositum fuit ei, quod significat *Salvatorem*. Hic, cum im- bueretur *sacro Baptismo*, 4. (*Sacramento novi Fœderis*) à *Johanne* præcursore suo, 5. in *Jordane* apparuit sacratissimum *Mysterium* Divinæ *Trinitatis*, *Patris* voce, 6. (quâ testabatur hunc esse *Filium* suum) & *Spiritu sancto* in specie *Colum- bæ*, 7. delabente cœlitus. Ab eo tempore, tricesimo anno ætatis suæ, usque an annum quartum, declaravit quis es- set, verbis & operibus præ se ferentibus Divinitatem, nec agnitus, nec acceptus a *Judæis*, ob voluntariam <u>paupertatem</u>. Captus tandem ab his (quum prius instituisset *Cœ-* | had first instituted the *Mys- tical Supper*, 8. *of his Body and Blood* for a Seal of the *new Covenant* and the remembrance of himself) carried to the *Judgment-seat of Pilate*, Governour under *Cæsar*, accused and con- demned as an innocent *Lamb*; and being fastned up- on a *Cross*, 9. he dyed, being sacrificed upon the Altar for the sins of the World. But when he had revived by his Divine Power, he rose again the third day out of the *Grave*, 10. and forty days af- ter being taken up from *Mount Olivet*, 11. into *Heaven*, 12. and returning thither whence he came, he vanished as it were, while the *Apos- tles*, 13. gazed upon him, to whom he sent his *Holy Spirit*, 14. from *Heaven*, the tenth day after his *Ascen- sion*,	nam *Mysticam*, 8. *Corporis & San- guinis sui*, in Sigillum *novi Fœderis*, & sui recorda- tionem) raptus ad *Tri- bunal Pilati*, Præfecti *Cæsarei*, accusatus & damnatus est *Agnus* innocentis- simus; actusque in *Crucem*, 9. mortem subiit, immolatus in arâ pro peccatis mun- di. Sed quum re- vixisset Divinâ suâ Vir- tute, resurrexit tertia die è *Sepulchro*, 10. & post dies XL. sublatus de *Monte Oliveti*, 11. in *Cœlum*, 12. & eo rediens unde venerat, quasi evanuit, *Apostolis*, 13. aspectantibus, quibus misit *Spiritum Sanc- tum*, 14. de *Cœlo*, decima die post *Ascensum*, ipsos vero,

CXLV.

Gentilism.

Gentilimus.

The Gentiles feigned to themselves near upon XIIM. Deities.	Gentiles finxerunt sibi prope XIIM. Numina.

The chief of them were
Jupiter, 1. President, and
petty-God of Heaven;
Neptune, 2. of the Sea;
Pluto, 3. of Hell;
Mars, 4. of War;
Apollo, 5. of Arts;
Mercury, 6. of Thieves, Merchants, and Eloquence;
Vulcan, (Mulciber) of Fire and Smiths;
Æolus, of Winds: and the most obscene of all the rest, Priapus.

Eorum præcipua erant
Jupiter, 1. Præses & Deaster cœli;
Neptunus, 2. Maris;
Pluto, 3. Inferni;
Mars, 4. Belli;
Apollo, 5. Artium;
Mercurius, 6. Furum, Mercatorum, & Eloquentiæ;
Vulcanus (Mulciber), Ignis & Fabrorum;
Æolus, Ventorum; & obscænissimus, Priapus.

They had also Womanly Deities: such as were
Venus, 7. the Goddess of Loves, and Pleasures, with her little son Cupid, 8.
Minerva (Pallas), with the nine Muses of Arts;
Juno, of Riches and Weddings;
Vesta, of Chastity;
Ceres, of Corn;
Diana, of Hunting, and Fortune;
and besides these Morbona, and Febris her self.

Habuerant etiam Muliebria Numina; qualia fuerunt
Venus, 7. Dea Amorum, & Voluptatum, cum filiolo Cupidine, 8.
Minerva (Pallas), cum novem Musis Artium;
Juno, Divitiarum & Nuptiarum;
Vesta, Castitatis;
Ceres, Frumentorum;
Diana, Venationum;
& Fortuna: quin & Morbona, ac Febris ipsa.

The Egyptians, instead of God worshipped all sorts of Beasts and Plants, and whatsoever they saw first in the morning.
The Philistines offered to Moloch, 9. their Children to be burnt alive.

Ægyptii, pro Deo colebant omne genus Animalium & Plantarum, & quicquid conspiciebantur primum mane.
Philistæi offerebant Molocho (Saturno), 9. Infantes cremandos vivos.

The Indians, 10. even to this day, worship the Devil, 11.

Indi, 10. etiamnum venerantur Cacodæmona, 11.

CXLVI.

Judaism.

Judaismus.

Yet the true Worship of the true God,

Verus tamen Cultus veri Dei,

remained with the Patriarchs, who lived before and after the Flood.
Amongst these, that Seed of the Woman, the Messias of the World, was promised to Abraham, the Founder of the Jews, the Father of them that believe:
and he (being called away from the Gentiles, with his Posterity, being marked with the Sacrament of Circumcision, 2. made a peculiar people, and Church of God.
Afterwards God gave his Law, written with his own Finger in Tables of Stone 5.
to this people 187 by Moses, 3. in Mount Sinai, 4

Furthermore he ordained the eating the Paschal Lamb, 6. and Sacrifices to be offered upon an Altar, 7. by Priests, 8. and Incense, 9. and commanded a Tabernacle, 10. with the Ark of the Covenant, 11. to be made:
and besides, a brazen Serpent, 12.

Aut quum igne corripiuntur, & vel ex incendio *pulveris tormentarii*, 4. homines ejiciuntur in ærem, vel exuruntur in mediis aquis, vel etiam desilientes in mare, suffocantur.
Navis fugitiva, 5. intercipitur ab *insequentibus*, 6. & capitur.

Urbs passura *Obsidionem*, primum provocatur per *Tubicinem*, 1. & invitatur ad *Depitionem*. Quod si abnuat facere, oppugnatur ab *Obsidentibus* & occupatur.

Vel muros per *Scalas*, 2. transcendendo, aut diruendo *Arietibus*, 3. aut demoliendo *Tormentis*, 4.

gins, 3. or demolishing them with *great Guns*, 4. or breaking through the Gates with a *Petarr*, 5. or casting *Granadoes*, 6. out of *Mortar-pieces*, 7. into the City, by *Engineers*, 8. (who lye behind *Leaguer-baskets*, 9.) or overthrowing it with *Mines* by *Pioneers*, 10.

They that are besieged defend themselves from the *Walls*, 11. with fire and stones, &c, or *break out by force*, 12.

A *City* that is taken by *Storm* is plundered, destroyed, and sometimes laid even with the ground. 183

CXLIV.
Religion.
Religio.

Godliness, 1. the Queen of Vertues,

vel dirumpendo portas *Exostra*, 5. vel ejaculando *Globos Tormentarios*, 6. e *Mortariis* (*balistis*), 7. in Urbem per *Balistarios*, 8. (qui latitant post *Gerras*, 9.) vel subvertendo *Cuniculis* per *Fossores*, 10.

Obsessi defendunt se de *Muris*, 11. ignibus, lapidibus, &c. aut *erumpunt*, 12.

Urbs vi expugnata, diriditur, exciditur, interdum equatur solo.

Pietas, 1. Regina Virtutum colit Deum, 4.

worshippeth God, 4. devoutly, the Knowledge of God being drawn either from the *Book of Nature*, 2. (for the work commendeth the Work-master) or from the *Book of Scripture*, 3. she meditateth upon his Commandments contained in the *Decalogue*, 5. and treading Reason under foot, that *Barking Dog*, 6. she giveth *Faith*, 7. and assent to the Word of God, and *calleth* upon him, 8. as a Helper in adversity.

Divine Services 184 are done in the *Church*, 9. in which are the *Quire*, 10. with the *Altar*, 11. the *Vestry*, 12. the *Pulpit*, 13. *Seats*, 14. *Galleries*, 15. and a *Font*, 16.

All men perceive that there is a God, but all men do not rightly know God.

Hence are divers *Religions* whereof IV. are

humiliter, Notitiâ Dei, haustâ vel ex *Libro Naturæ*, 2. (nam opus commendat Artificem) vel ex *Libro Scripturæ*, 3. recolit Mandata ejus comprehensa in *Decalogo*, 5. & conculcans Rationem, *oblatrantem Canem*, 6. præbet *Fidem*, 7. & assensum Verbo Dei, eumque *invocat*, 8. ut Opitulatorem in adversis.

Officia Divina fiunt in *Templo*, 9. in quo est *Penetrale* (Adytum, 10.) cum *Altari*, 11. *Sacrarium*, 12. *Suggestus*, 13. *Subsellia*, 14. *Ambones*, 15. & *Baptisterium*, 16.

Omnes homines sentiunt esse Deum, sed non omnes rectè nôrunt Deum.

Hinc diversæ *Religiones* quarum IV. nu-

Bullets, 33.
out of a *Bullet-bag*, 34.
and with *Gun-powder*
out of a *Bandalier*, 35.

CXL.

The Camps.

Castra.

178 When a *Design* is undertaken
the *Camp*, 1. is pitched
and the *Tents*
of *Canvas*, 2. or *Straw*, 3.
are fastned with *Stakes*;
and they entrench them about
for security's sake,
with *Bulwarks*, 4.
and *Ditches*, 5.
Sentinels, 6. are also set;
and *Scouts*, 7. are sent out.

Sallyings out, 8.
are made for Forage
and Plunder-sake,
where
they often cope with
the *Enemy*, 9. in skirmishing.

The *Pavilion*
of the *Lord General* is in
the midst of the *Camp*, 10.

33.
è *Theca bombardica*, 34.
& *Pulvere nitrato*
è *Pyxide pulveraria*, 35.

Expeditione susceptâ,
Castra, 1. locantur
& *Tentoria Lintea*, 2. vel *Stramentis*, 3. figuntur *Paxillis*;
eaque circumdant,
securitatis gratiâ
Aggeribus, 4.
& *Fossis*, 5.
Excubiæ, 6. constituuntur;
& *Exploratores*, 7. emittuntur.

Excursiones, 8.
fiunt Pabulationis
& Prædæ causâ,
ubi
sæpius confligitur cum
Hostibus, 9. velitando

Tentorium summi Imperatoris est in
medio *Castrorum*, 10.

CXLI.

The Army and the Fight.

Acies & Prœlium.

When the *Battel* 179 is to be fought
the *Army* is set in order,
and divided into
the *Front*, 1.
the *Rere*, 2.
and the *Wings*, 3.
The *Foot*, 4.
are intermixed
with the *Horse*, 5.
That is divided into *Companies*,
this into *Troops*.
These carry *Banners*, 6.
those *Flags*, 7.
in the midst of them.

Their Officers are, *Corporals*, *Ensigns*,
Lieutenants, *Captains*, 8.
Commanders of the Horse, 9.
Lieutenant *Colonels*,
Colonels,
and he that is the chief of all,
the *General*.
The *Drummers*, 10.
and the *Drumslades*, 11.
as also the *Trumpeters*, 12.
call to Arms,
and inflame the Soldier.

Quando *Pugna* committenda est,
Acies instruitur,
& dividitur in *Frontem*, 1.
Tergum, 2.
& *Alas* (*Cornua*), 3.
Peditatus, 4.
intermiscetur *Equitatui*, 5.
Ille distinguitur in *Centurias*,
hic in *Turmas*.
Illæ in medio ferunt *Vexilla*, 6.
hæ *Labara*, 7.

Eorum Præfecti sunt,
Decuriones, *Signiferi*,
Vicarii, *Centuriones*, 8.
Magistri Equitum, 9.
Tribuni,
Chiliarchæ,
& summus omnium
Imperator.
Tympanistæ, 10.
& *Tympanotribæ*, 11.
ut & *Tubicines*, 12.
vocant ad Arma
& inflammant Militem.

At the first Onset
the *Muskets*, 13.
and
Ordnance, 14. are shot off.
Afterwards they fight, 15.
hand to hand
with *Pikes* and *Swords*.
They that are overcome
are *slain*, 16.
or taken prisoners
or *run away*, 17.
They that are for the *Reserve*, 18.
come upon them 180 out of their
places where they lay in wait.
The *Carriages*, 1
are plundered.

CXLII.

The Sea-Fight.

Pugna Navalis.

A *Sea-fight*
is terrible,
when huge *Ships*
like *Castles*,
run one upon another
with their *Beaks*,
or shatter one another
with their *Ordnance*, 2.
and so being bored thorow
they drink in
their own Destruction,
and are *sunk*, 3.

Rex, 1.
sedet in suo Solio, 2.
in regio splendore,
magnifico
Habitu, 3.
redimitus Diademate, 4.
tenens Sceptrum, 5.
manu,
stipatus
frequentiâ
Aulicorum.
inter hos primarii
sunt Cancellarius, 6.
cum Consiliariis
& Secretariis,
Præfectus Prætorii, 7.
Aulæ Magister, 8.
Pocillator (pincerna), 9.
Dapifer, 10.
Thesaurarius, 11.
Archi-Cubicularius, 12.
& Stabuli Magister, 13.
Subordinantur
his
Nobiles Aulici, 14.
Nobile Famulitium, 15.
cum Cubiculari-

with the *Chamberlains*,
and *Lacquies*, 16.
the *Guard*, 17.
with their *Attendance*.
He solemnly giveth Audience
to the *Ambassadors*
of Foreign Princes, 18.
He sendeth
his *Vice-gerents*,
Deputies,
Governors, Treasurers,
and *Ambassadors*
to other places,
to whom he sendeth
new *Commissions*
ever and anon
by the *Posts*, 19.
The *Fool*, 20.
maketh Laughter
by his toysom Actions.
176

CXXXIX.

The Soldier.

Miles.

If we be to make War
Soldiers are lifted, 1.
Their *Arms* are
a *Head-piece*, 2.
(which is adorned
with a
Crest) and the *Armour*,

is,
& *Cursoribus*, 16.
Stipatores, 17.
cum *Satellitio*.

Solemniter recipit
Legatos
exterorum, 18.

Ablegat
Vicarios suos,
Administratores,
Præfectos, Quæstores,
& *Legatos*,
aliorsum,
quibus mittit
Mandata nova
subinde
per *Veredarios*, 19.
Morio, 20.
movet Risum
ludicris Actionibus.

Si bellandum est
scribuntur
Milites. 1.

Horum *Arma*
sunt,
Galea (Cassis, 2.)
(quæ ornatur
Cristâ) & Armatura,

whose parts are a
Collar, 3.
a *Breast-plate*, 4.
Arm-pieces, 5.
Leg-pieces, 6.
Greaves, 7.
with a *Coat of Mail*, 8.
and a *Buckler*, 9.
these are the defensive Arms.

The offensive are
a *Sword*, 10.
a *two-edged Sword*, 11.
a *Falchion*, 12.
which are put up into
a *Scabbard*, 13.
and are girded with
a *Girdle*, 14. or *Belt*, 15.
177 (a *Scarf*, 16.
serveth for ornament)
a *two handed-Sword*, 17.
and a *Dagger*, 18.
In these is the
Haft, 19.
with the *Pummel*, 20.
and the *Blade*, 21.
having a *Point*, 22.
in the middle are
the *Back*, 23. and
the *Edge*, 24.
The other
Weapons are
a *Pike*, 25. a *Halbert*, 26.
(in which is the
Haft, 27.
and the *Head*, 28.)
a *Club*, 29. and a
Whirlebat, 30.
They fight at a distance
with *Muskets*, 31.
and *Pistols*, 32.
which
are charged with

cujus partes
Torquis ferreus, 3.
Thorax, 4.
Brachialia, 5.
Ocreæ ferreæ, 6.
Manicæ, 7.
cum *Lorica*, 8.
& *Scuto*
(Clypeo), 9.
hæc sunt Arma
defensiva.

Offensiva sunt
Gladius, 10.
Framea, 11.
& *Acinaces*, 12.
qui reconduntur
Vaginâ, 13.
accinguntur
Cingulo, 14. vel
Baltheo, 15.
(*Fascia militaris*, 16.
inservit ornatui)
Romphæa, 17.
& *Pugio*, 18.

In his est
Manubrium, 19.
cum *Pomo*, 20.
& *Verutum*, 21.
Cuspidatum, 22.
in medio
Dorsum, 23. &
Acies, 24.

Reliqua arma
sunt
Hasta, 25. Bipennis, 26.
(in quibus
Hastile, 27.
& *Mucro*, 28.)
Clava, 29. &
Cæstus, 30.

Pugnatur eminùs
Bombardis
(Sclopetis), 31.
& *Sclopis*, 32.
quæ
onerantur *Globis*,

upon a *Board*, 3. marked with figures, and this is *Dice-players* game at *casting Lots*.

Men play by *Luck* and *Skill* at *Tables*, in a *pair of Tables*, 4. 171 and at *Cards*, 5.

We play at *Chesse* on a *Chesse-board*, 6. where only art beareth the sway.

The most ingenious Game is the Game of *Chesse*, 7. wherein as it were two Armies fight together in Battel.

idque est *Ludas Sortilegii Aleatorum*.

Sorte & *Arte* luditur *Calculis* in *Alveo aleatorio*, 4. & *Chartis lusoriis*, 5.

Ludimus *Abaculis* in *Abaco*, 6. ubi sola ars regnat.

Ingeniosissimus Ludus est Ludus *Latrunculorum*, 7. quo veluti duo Exercitus confligunt Prælio.

CXXXV.
Races.
Cursus Certamina.

Boys exercise themselves by running, either upon the *Ice*, 1. in *Scrick-shoes*, 2. where they are carried also upon *Sleds*, 3. or in the open Field, making a *Line*, 4. which he that desireth to win,

Pueri exercent se cursu, sive super *Glaciem*, 1. *Diabetris*, 2. ubi etiam vehuntur *Trahis*, 3. sive in Campo, designantes *Lineam*, 4. quam qui vincere cupit debet attingere,

ought to touch, but not to run beyond it.

Heretofore *Runners*, 5. run betwixt *Rails*, 6. 172 to the *Goal*, 7. and he that toucheth it first receiveth the *Prize*, 8. from *him that gave the prize*, 9.

At this day *Tilting* (or the quintain) is used, (where a *Hoop*, 11. is struck at with a *Truncheon*, 10.) instead of *Horse-races*, which are grown out of use.

CXXXVI.
Boys Sport.
Ludi Pueriles.

Boys use to play either with *Bowling-stones* 1. or throwing a *Bowl*, 2. at *Nine-pins*, 3. or striking a *Ball*, through a *Ring*, 5. with a *Bandy*, 4. or scourging a *Top*, 6. with a *Whip*, 7. 173 or shooting with a *Trunk*, 8.

at non ultrâ procurrere.

Olim decurrebant *Cursores*, 5. inter *Cancellos*, 6. ad *Metam*, 7. & qui primum contingebat eam, accipiebat *Brabeum*, (*præmium*), 8. à *Brabeuta*, 9.

Hodie *Hastiludia* habentur, (ubi *Circulus*, 11. petitur *Lancea*, 10.) loco *Equiriorum*, quæ abierunt in desuetudinem.

Pueri solent ludere vel *Globis fictilibus*, 1. vel jactantes *Globum*, 2. ad *Conas*, 3. vel mittentes *Sphærulam* per *Annulum*, 5. *Clava*, 4. versantes *Turbinem*, 6. *Flagello*, 7.

and a *Bow*, 9. or going upon *Stilts*, 10. or tossing and swinging themselves upon a *Merry-tott*, 11.

CXXXVII.
The Kingdom and
Regnum & Regio

Many *Cities* and *Villages* make a *Region* and a *Kingdom*.

The *King* or *Prince* resideth in the chief *City*, 1. the *Noblemen*, *Lords*, and *Earls* dwell in the *Castles*, 2. that lie about it; the *Country People* dwell in *Villages*, 3.

174 He hath his *toll-places* upon *navigable Rivers*, 4. and *high-Roads*, 5. where *Portage* and *Tollage* is exacted of them that sail or travel.

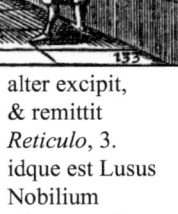

& plaudit,
si quid arridet.

Præstigiator, 1.
facit varia
Spectacula,
volubilitate
corporis,
deambulando
manibus,
saliendo
per *Circulum*, 2. &c.
Interdum etiam
tripudiat, 4.
Larvatus.

Agyrta, 3.
facit *præstigias*
è *Marsupio*.

Funambulus, 5.
graditur &
saltat
super *Funem*,
tenens *Halterem*, 6.
manu;
aut suspendit
se
manu vel *pede*, 7. &c.

Pugiles
congrediuntur
Duello
in *Palestra*,

Swords, 1.
or *Pikes*, 2.
and *Halberds*, 3.
or *Short-swords*, 4.
or *Rapiers*, 5.
having balls at the point
(lest they wound one another mortally)
or with *two edged-Swords*
and a *Dagger*, 6.
together.

169 *Wrestlers*, 7.
(among the Romans
in time past were
nayked
and anointed with Oyl)
take hold of one another
and strive whether
can throw the other,
especially
by *tripping up his heels*, 8.

Hood-winked Fencers, 9.
fought with their
fists
in a ridiculous
strife,
to wit, with their
Eyes covered.

CXXXIII.

Tennis-play.

Ludus Pilæ.

In a *Tennis Court*, 1.
they play with a

decertantes vel
Gladiis, 1.
vel *Hastilibus*, 2.
& *Bipennibus*, 3.
vel *Semispathis*, 4.
vel *Ensibus*, 5.
mucronem
obligatis,
(ne lædet
lethaliter)
vel *Frameis*
& *Pugione*, 6.
simul.

Luctatores, 7.
(apud Romanos
olim nudi
& inuncti Oleo)
prehendunt se
invicem
& annituntur
uter
alterum
prosternere possit,
præprimis
supplantando, 8.

Andabatæ, 9.
pugnabant pugnis
ridiculo certamine,
nimirum Oculis
obvelatis.

In *Sphæristerio*, 1.
luditur *Pilâ*, 2.
quam alter mittit,

Ball, 2.
which one
throweth,
and another
taketh,
and sendeth it
back
with a *Racket*, 3.
170 and that is
the Sport
of Noble Men
to stir their
Body.

A *Wind-ball*, 4.
being filled with
Air,
by means of a
Ventil,
is tossed to and
fro
with the *Fist*, 5.
in the open Air.

CXXXIV.

Dice-play.

Ludus Aleæ.

We play with
Dice, 1.
either they that
throw
the most take up
all;
or we throw them
through a *Casting-box*, 2.

alter excipit,
& remittit
Reticulo, 3.
idque est Lusus
Nobilium
ad commotionem
Corporis.

Follis (pila
magna), 4.
distenta Aere
ope *Epistomii*,
reverberbatur
Pugno, 5.
sub Dio.

Tesseris (*talis*), 1.
ludimus
vel *Plistobolindam*;
vel immittimus illas
per *Frittillum*, 2.
in *Tabellam*, 3.
notatam numeris,

weigheth things by hanging them on a *Hook*, 13. and the *Weight*, 14. opposite to them which in (a) weigheth just as much as the thing, in (b) twice so much in (c) thrice so much, &c.	pendendo illas *Unco*, 13. & *Pondus*, 14. ex opposito, quod in (a) æquiponderat rei, in (b) bis tantum, in (c) ter, &c.

CXXVIII.

Physick.

Ars Medica.

The *Patient*, 1. sendeth for a *Physician*, 2. 164 who feeleth his *Pulse*, 3, and looketh upon his *Water*, 4. and then prescribeth a *Receipt* in a *Bill*, 5.	*Ægrotans*, 1. accersit *Medicum*, 2. qui tangit ipsius *Arteriam*, 3. & inspicit *Urinam*, 4. tum præscribit *Medicamentum* in *Schedula*, 5.
That is made ready by an *Apothecary*, 6. in a *Apothecaries Shop*, 7. where *Drugs* are kept in *Drawers*, 8. *Boxes*, 9. and *Gally-pots*, 10.	Istud paratur à *Pharmacopæo*, 6. in *Pharmacopolio*, 7. ubi *Pharmaca* adservantur in *Capsulis*, 8. *Pyxidibus*, 9. & *Lagenis*, 10.
And it is either a *Potion*, 11. or *Powder*, 12. or *Pills*, 13. or *Trochisks*, 14. or an *Electuary*, 15.	*Estque* vel *Potio*, 11. vel *Pulvis*, 12. vel *Pillulæ*, 13. vel *Pastilli*, 14. vel *Electuarium*, 15.
Diet and *Prayer*, 16. is the best *Physick*. The *Chirurgeon*, 18. cureth *Wounds* 17. and *Ulcers*, with *Plasters*, 19. 165	*Diæta* & *Oratio*, 16. est optima *Medicina*. *Chirurgus*, 18. curat *Vulnera*, 17. & *Ulcera*, *Spleniis* (emplastris), 19.

CXXIX.

A Burial.

Sepultura.

Dead Folks heretofore were burned, and their Ashes put into an *Urn*, 1.	*Defuncti* olim cremabantur, & *Cineres* recondebantur in *Urna*, 1.
We enclose our dead *Folks* in a *Coffin*, 2. lay them upon a *Bier*, 3. and see they be carried out in a *Funeral Pomp* towards the *Church-yard*, 4. where they are laid in a *Grave*, 6. by the *Bearers*, 5. and are interred; this is covered with a *Grave-stone*, 7. and is adorned with *Tombs*, 8. and *Epitaphs*, 9. 166 As the Corps go along *Psalms* are sung, and the *Bells* are rung, 10.	Nos includimus nostros *Demortuos* *Loculo*, (*Capulo*), 2. imponimus *Feretro*, 3. & curamus efferri *Pompâ Funebri* versus *Cæmeterium*, 4. ubi inferuntur, *Sepulchro*, 6. a *Vespillonibus*, 5. & humantur; hoc tegitur *Cippo*, 7. & ornatur a *Grave-stone*, 7.

CXXX.

A Stage-play.

Ludus Scenicus.

In a *Play-house*, (which is trimmed with *Hangings*, 2. and covered with *Curtains*, 3.) *Comedies* and *Tragedies* are acted, wherein memorable things are represented; as here, the *History* of the *Prodigal Son*, 4. and his *Father*, 5. by whom he is entertain'd, being return'd home. The *Players* act being in disguise; the *Fool*, 6. maketh Jests.

167 The chief of *Spectators* sit in the *Gallery* the common sort stand on the *Ground*, 8.

CXXVI.

Merchandizing.

Mercatura.

Wares brought from other places are either exchanged in an *Exchange*, 1.
or exposed to sale in *Warehouses*, 2.
and they are sold for *Money*, 3.
being either measured with an *Eln*, 4.
or weighed in a *pair of Balances*, 5.

Shop-keepers, 6.
Pedlars, 7.
and *Brokers*, 8.
would also be called *Merchants*, 9.

The *Seller* braggeth of a thing that is to be sold, and setteth the rate of it, and how much it may be sold for.

The *Buyer*, 10. cheapneth and offereth the price.

If any one bid *against him*, 11.

Merces, aliunde allatæ, aliunde vel commutantur in *Domo Commerciorum*, 1.
vel exponuntur venum in *Tabernis Mercimoniorum*, 2.
& venduntur pro *Pecuniâ* (monetâ), 3.
vel mensuratæ *Ulnâ*, 4.
vel ponderatæ *Libra*, 5.

Tabernarii, 6.
Circumforanei, 7.
& *Scrutarii*, 8.
etiam volunt dici *Mercatores*, 9.

Venditor ostentat rem promercalem, & indicat pretium, quanti liceat.

Emptor, 10. licetur, & pretium offert.

Si quis contralicetur, 11.
ei res addicitur

the thing is delivered to him that promiseth the most.

qui pollicetur plurimum.

CXXVII. *

Measures and Weights.

Mensuræ & Pondera.

We measure things that hang together with an *Eln*, 1.
liquid things with a *Gallon*, 2.
and dry things by a *two-bushel Measure*, 3.

We try the heaviness of things by *Weights*, 4.
and *Balances*, 5.

In this is first the *Beam*, 6. in the midst whereof is a little *Axle-tree*, 7. above the *cheeks* and the *hole*, 8.
in which the *Needle*, 9. moveth it self to and fro:
on both sides are the *Scales*, 10. hanging by little *Cords*, 11.

The *Brasiers balance*, 12.

Res continuas metimur *Ulnâ*, 1.
liquidas *Congio*, 2.
aridas *Medimno*, 3.

Gravitatem rerum experimur *Ponderibus*, 4.
& *Libra* (bilance), 5.

In hâc primò est *Jugum* (Scapus), 6.
in cujus medio *Axiculus*, 7. superiùs *trutina* & *agina*, 8.
in quâ *Examen*, 9.
sese agitat: utrinque sunt *Lances*, 10. pendentes *Funiculis*, 11.

Statera, 12. ponderat res, sus-

CXXIII.

The inward parts of a City.

Interiora Urbis.

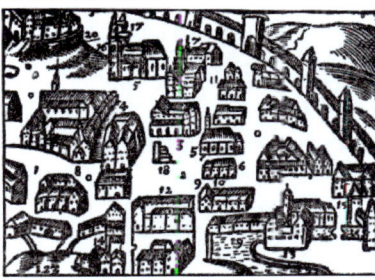

Within the City are	Intra urbem sunt
Streets, 1.	Plateæ (Vici), 1.
paved with Stones;	stratæ Lapidibus;
Market-places, 2.	Fora, 2.
(in some places with	(alicubi cum
Galleries), 3.	Porticibus), 3.
and narrow Lanes, 4.	& Angiportus, 4.
The Publick Buildings are in the middle of the City,	Publica ædificia sunt in medio Urbis.
the Church, 5.	Templum, 5.
the School, 6.	Schola, 6.
the Guild-Hall, 7.	Curia, 7.
the Exchange, 8.	Domus Mercaturæ, 8.
About the Walls and the Gates are the Magazine, 9.	Circa Mœnia, & Portas Armamentarium, 9.
the Granary, 10.	Granarium, 10.
Inns, Ale-houses, Cooks-shops, 11.	Diversoria, Popinæ, & Cauponæ, 11.
the Play-house, 12.	Theatrum, 12.
and the Spittle, 13.	Nosodochium, 13.
In the by-places are Houses of Office, 14.	In recessibus, Foricæ (Cloacæ), 14.
and the Prison, 15.	& Custodia (Carcer), 15.
In the chief Steeple is the Clock, 16. and the Watchmans Dwelling, 17.	In turre primariâ est Horologium, 16. & habitatio Vigilum, 17.
In the Streets are Wells, 18.	In Plateis sunt Putei, 18.
The River, 19. or Beck, runneth about the City, serveth to wash away the filth.	Fluvius, 19. vel Rivus, interfluens Urbem, inservit eluendis sordibus.
The Tower, 20. standeth in the highest part of the City.	Arx, 20. extat in summo Urbis.

CXXIV.

Judgment.

Judicium.

The best Law, is a quiet agreement, made either by themselves, betwixt whom the sute is, or by an Umpire.	Optimum Jus, est placida conventio, facta vel ab ipsis, inter quos lis est vel ab Arbitro.
If this do not proceed, they come into Court, 1. (heretofore they judg'd in the Market-place; at this day in the Moot-hall) in which the Judge, 2. sitteth with his Assessors, 3.	Hæc si non procedit, venitur in Forum, 1. (olim judicabant in Foro, hodiè in Prætorio) cui Judex (Prætor), 2. præsidet cum Assessoribus, 3.
the Clerk, 4. taketh their Votes in writing.	
The Plaintiff, 5. accuseth the Defendant, 6. and produceth Witnesses, 7. against him.	
The Defendant excuseth himself by a Counsellor, 8. whom the Plaintiff's Counsellor, contradicts.	
Then the Judge pronounceth Sentence, acquitting the innocent, and condemning him that is guilty, to a Punishment, or a Fine, or Torment.	

CXXV.

The Tormenting

Supplicia Malefac

Malefactors, 1. are brought from the Prison, (where they are wont to be tortured) by Serjeants, 2. or dragg'd with a Horse, 15. to place of Execu-

Pater, 1. generat
& *Mater*, 2. parit
Filios, 3. & *Fil-
as*, 4.
(aliquando
Gemellos).

Infans, 5.
involvitur
Fasciis, 6.
reponitur in *Cu-
nas*, 7.
lactatur a matre
Uberibus, 8.
& nutritur *Pap-
pis*, 9.
Deinde discit
incedere *Seperas-
so*, 10.
ludit *Crepundiis*,
11.
& incipit fari.

Crescente ætate,
adsuescit
Pietati, 12.
& *Labori*, 13.
& castigatur, 14.
si non sit
morigerus.

Liberi debent
Parentibus
Cultum & *Offici-
um*.
Pater sustentat
Liberos,
laborando, 15.

CXXI.

The Society betwixt Masters and Servants.

Societas herilis.

The *Master*
(*the goodman of
the House*), 1.
hath *Men-ser-
vants*, 2.
154 the *Mistress*
(*the good wife of
the House*), 3.
Maidens, 4.
They appoint
these
their *Work*, 6.
and divide
them their tasks,
5. which
are faithfully to be
done by them
without murmur-
ing
and loss:
for which
their *Wages*,
and *Meat* and
Drink
is allowed them.

A *Servant* was
heretofore
a *Slave*,
over whom the
Master
had power of life
and death.
At this day the
poorer sort
serve in a free
manner,
being hired for
Wages.

Herus
(*Pater familias*),
1.
habet *Famulos*
(*Servos*), 2.
Hera
(*Mater familias*),
3.
Ancillas, 4.
Illi mandant his
Opera, 6.
& distribuunt
Laborum Pensa,
5. quæ
ab his fideliter
sunt exsequenda
sine murmure
& dispendio;
pro quo
Merces
& *Alimonia*
præbentur ipsis.

Servus olim erat
Mancipium,
in quem Domino
potestas fuit vitæ
& necis.
Hodiè pauperi-
ores
serviunt liberè,
conducti mer-
cede.

CXXII.

A City.

Urbs.

Of many Houses
is made a *Village*,
1.
155 or a *Town*, or
a *City*, 2.
That and this are
fenced
and begirt with a
Wall, 3.
a *Trench*, 4.
Bulwarks, 5.
and *Pallisadoes*,
6.
Within the Walls
is
the *void Place*, 7.
without, the
Ditch, 8.
In the Walls are
Fortresses, 9.
and *Towers*, 10.
Watch-Towers,
11. are
upon the higher
places.
The entrance into
a City
is made out of the
Suburbs, 12.
through *Gates*,
13.
over the *Bridge*,
14.
The *Gate*
hath a *Portcullis*,
15.
a *Draw-bridge*,
16.
two-leaved
Doors, 17.
Locks and *Bolts*,

Ex multis
Domibus
fit *Pagus*, 1.
vel *Oppidum*, vel
Urbs, 2.
Istud & hæc muni-
untur
& cinguntur
Mœnibus (*Muro*),
3.
Vallo, 4.
Aggeribus, 5.
& *Vallis*, 6.
Intra muros est
Pomœrium, 7.
extrà, *Fossa*, 8.

In mœnibus sunt
Propugnacula, 9.
& *Turres*, 10.
Specula, 11. ex-
tant
in editioribus
locis.
Ingressus in
Urbem
fit ex *Suburbio*,
12.
per *Portam*, 13.
super *Pontem*, 14.

Porta
habet *Cataractas*,
15.
*Pontem versa-
tilem*, 16.
Valvas, 17.
Claustra &
Repagula,

than of *Beauty* or *Portion*.
Afterwards, he doth not betroth her to himself closely, but entreateth for her as a *Woer*, first to the *Father*, 1. and then the *Mother*, 2. or the *Guardians*, or *Kinsfolks*, by such *as help to make the match*, 3.
When she is espous'd to him, he becometh the *Bridegroom*, 4. and she the *Bride*, 5. and the *Contract* is made, and an *Instrument* of *Dowry* 6. is written.
At the last the *Wedding* is made, where they are joined together by the *Priest*, 7. giving their *Hands*, 8. one to another, and *Wedding-rings*, 9. then they feast with the witnesses that are invited.
After this they are called *Husband* and *Wife*; when she is dead he becometh a *Widower*.

quàm *Formæ* aut *Dotis*.
Posthæc, non clam despondet sibi eam, sed ambit, ut *Procus*, apud *Patrem*, 1. & *Matrem*, 2. vel apud *Tutores*, & *Cognatos*, per *Pronubos*, 3.
Eâ sibi desponsâ, fit *Sponsus*, 4. & ipsa *Sponsa*, 5. fiuntque *Sponsalia*, & scribitur *Instrumentum Dotale*, 6.
Tandem fiunt *Nuptiæ* ubi copulantur à *Sacerdote*, 7. datis *Manibus*, 8. ultro citroque, & *Annulis Nuptialibus*, 9. tum epulantur cum invitatis testibus.
Abhinc dicuntur *Maritus* & *Uxor*, hâc mortuâ ille fit *Viduus*.

CXIX.

The Tree of Consanguinity.

Arbor Consanguinitatis.

In *Consanguinity* there touch a *Man*, 1.

Hominem, 1. Consanguinitate attingunt,

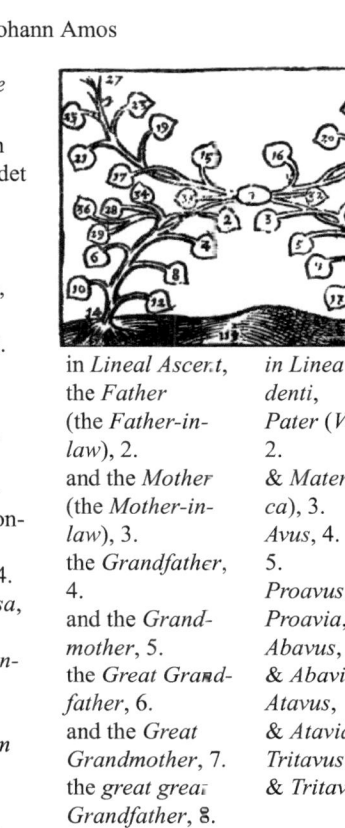

in *Lineal Ascent*, the *Father* (the *Father-in-law*), 2. and the *Mother* (the *Mother-in-law*), 3. the *Grandfather*, 4. and the *Grandmother*, 5. the *Great Grandfather*, 6. and the *Great Grandmother*, 7. the *great great Grandfather*, 8. the *great great Grandmother*, 9. the *great great Grandfather's Father*, 10. the *great great Grandmother's Mother*, 11. the *great great Grandfather's Grandfather*, 12. the *great great Grandmother's Grandmother*, 13.
Those beyond these are called *Ancestors*, 14.14.
In a *Lineal descent*, the *Son* (the *son-in-law*), 15. and the *Daughter*, (the *Daughter-in-law*), 16. the *Nephew*, 17. and the *Neece*, 18. the *Nephews Son*, 19.

in *Linea ascendenti*, *Pater* (*Vitricus*), 2. & *Mater* (*Noverca*), 3. *Avus*, 4. & *Avia*, 5. *Proavus*, 6. & *Proavia*, 7. *Abavus*, 8. & *Abavia*, 9. *Atavus*, 10. & *Atavia*, 11 *Tritavus*, 12. & *Tritavia*, 13.

Ulteriores dicuntur Majores, 14.14.
In *Linea descendenti*, *Filius* (*Privignus*), 15. & *Filia* (*Privigna*), 16. *Nepos*, 17. & *Neptis*, 18. *Pronepos*, 19. & *Proneptis*, 26. *Abnepos*, 21. &

and the *Nephews Daughter*, 20. the *Nephews Nephew*, 21. and the *Neeces Neece*, 22. the *Nephews Nephews Son*, 23. the *Neeces Neece Daughter*, 24 the *Nephews Nephews Nephew*, 25. the *Neeces Neece Neece*, 26.
Those beyond these are called *Posterity*, 27.27.
In a *Collateral Line* are the *Uncle by the Fathers side*, 28. and the *Aunt by the Fathers side*, 29. the *Uncle by the Mothers side*, 30. and the *Aunt by the Mothers side*, 31. the *Brother*, 32. and the *Sister*, 33 the *Brothers Son*, 34. the *Sisters Son*, 35 and the *Cousin by the Brother and Sister*, 36.

CXX.

The Society between Children.

Societas Parenta

Married Persons (by the blessing of God) have *issue*, and become *Parents*.

alteri parti;
Tenens dextrâ
Gladium, 5.
& *Frænum*, 6.
ad puniendum
& coërcendum
malos;

Præterea,
Stateram, 7.
cujus *dextræ*
Lanci, 8.
Merita,
Sinistræ, 9.
Præmia imposita,
sibi invicem exequantur,
atque ita boni
incitantur ad
virtutem,
ceu *Calcaribus*,
10.
In *Contractibus*,
11.
candidè agatur:
stetur
Pactis &
Promissis;
Depositum,
& *Mutuum*,
reddantur:
nemo *expiletur*,
12.
aut *lædatur*, 13.
suum cuique
tribuatur:
hæc sunt præcepta
Justitiæ.

Talia
prohibentur,
quinto & septimo Dei
Præcepto,
& merito puniuntur
Cruce ac *Rotâ*,
14.

CXVII.
Liberality.
Liberalitas.

Liberality, 1.
keepeth a mean
about *Riches*,
which she honestly
seeketh,
that she may have
somewhat to bestow
on them that *want*,
2.

She *cloatheth*, 3.
nourisheth, 4.
and *enricheth*, 5.
these
with a *chearful*
countenance, 6.
and a *winged*
hand, 7.

She submitteth her
wealth, 8. to her
self,
not her self to it,
as the *covetous*
man, 9. doth,
who hath,
that he may have,
and is not the
Owner,
but the *Keeper* of
his goods,
and being unsatiable,
always *scrapeth*
together, 10.
with his Nails.
148 Moreover he
spareth
and keepeth,
hoarding up, 11.
that he may always have.

Liberalitas, 1.
servat modum
circa *Divitias*,
quas honestè
quærit
ut habeat
quod largiatur
Egenis, 2.

Hos *vestit*, 3.
nutrit, 4.
ditat, 5.
Vultu hilari, 6.
& *Manu alatâ*, 7.

Subjicit
opes, 8. sibi,
non se illis,
ut *Avarus*, 9.
qui habet,
ut habeat,
& non est *Possessor*
sed *Custos* bonorum suorum,
& insatiabilis,
semper *corradit*,
10.
Unguibus suis.

Sed & parcit
& adservat,
occludendo, 11.
ut semper habeat.

But the *Prodigal*,
12.
badly spendeth
things well gotten,
and at the last
wanteth.

At *Prodigus*, 12.
malè disperdit
benè parta,
ac tandem eget.

CXVIII.
Society betwixt Man and Wife.
Societas Conjugalis.

Marriage
was appointed by
God
in Paradise,
for mutual *help*,
and the *Propagation*
of mankind.

Matrimonium
institutum est à
Deo
in Paradiso,
ad mutuum *adjutorium*,
& *propagationem*
generis humani.

A *young man* (a single man)
being to be married,
should be furnished
either with *Wealth*,
or a *Trade* and *Science*,
149 which may
serve
for getting a living;
that he may be able
to maintain a *Family*.

Vir Juvenis
(*Cœlebs*)
conjugium initurus,
instructus sit
aut *Opibus*,
aut *Arte* & *Scientiâ*,
quæ sit
de pane lucrando;
ut possit
sustentare *Familiam*.

Then he chooseth
himself
a *Maid* that is *Marriageable*,
(or a *Widow*)
whom he loveth;
nevertheless a
greater Regard
is to be had of
Virtue,
and *Honesty*,

Deinde eligit
sibi
Virginem Nubilem,
(aut *Viduam*)
quam adamat;
ubi tamen major ratio
habenda *Virtutis*
& *Honestatis*,

of *Sufferance*: and keepeth off the *Passions*, the enemies of quietness with the *Sword*, 5. of *Valour*.

propellit *Affectus*, hostes Euthymiæ gladio, 5. *Virtutis*.

CXIV.

Patience.

Patientia.

Patience, 1. endureth *Calamities*, 2. 143 and *Wrongs*, 3. meekly like a *Lamb*, 4. as the Fatherly *chastisement of God*, 5.
In the meanwhile she leaneth upon the *Anchor of Hope*, 6. (as a *Ship*, 7. tossed by waves in the Sea) *she prayeth to God*, 8. weeping, and expecteth the *Sun*, 10. after *cloudy weather*, 9. suffering evils, and hoping better things.
On the contrary, the *impatient person*, 11. waileth, lamenteth, *rageth against himself*, 12. grumbleth like a

Patientia, 1. tolerat *Calamitates*, 2. & *Injurias*, 3. humiliter ut *Agnus*, 4. tanquam paternam ferulam Dei, 5.
Interim innititur *Spei Anchoræ*, 6. (ut *Navis*, 7. fluctuans mari) Deo supplicat, 8. illacrymando, & expectat Phœbum, 10. post *Nubila*, 9. ferens mala, sperans meliora.

Contra, *Impatiens*, 11. plorat, lamentatur, debacchatur, 12. in seipsum, obmurmurat ut *Canis*, 13.

Dog, 13. and yet doth no good; at the last he despaireth, and becometh his own *Murtherer*, 14.
Being full of rage he desireth to revenge wrongs. 144

CXV.

Humanity.

Humanitas.

Men are made for one another's *good*; therefore let them be kind.

Be thou sweet and lovely in thy *Countenance*, 1. gentle and civil in thy *Behaviour* and *Manners*, 2. affable and true spoken with thy *Mouth*, 3. affectionate and *candid* in thy *Heart*, 4. So love, and so shalt thou be loved; and there will be a mutual *Friendship*, 5. as that of *Turtledoves*, 6. hearty, gentle,

& tamen nil proficit; tandem desperat, & fit *Autochir*, 14.

Furibundus cupit vindicare injurias.

Homines facti sunt ad mutua *commoda*; ergò sint *humani*.

Sis suavis & amabilis *Vultu*, 1. comis & urbanus *Gestu* ac *Moribus*, 2. affabilis & verax, *Ore*, 3. candens & candidus *Corde*, 4. Sic ama, sic amaberis; & fiat mutua *Amicitia*, 5. ceu *Turturum*, 6. concors, mansueta,

and wishing well both parts. Froward Men are hateful, teasty, unpleasant. 145 contentious, angry, 7. cruel, 8. and implacable, (rather Wolves and Lions, than Men) and such as fall out among themselves hereupon they fight in a *Duel*, 9.

Envy, 10. wishing ill to others pineth away her self.

CXVI.

Justice.

Justitia.

Justice, 1 is painted, sitting on a *square stone*, 2. for she ought to be immoveable; with *hood-winked eyes*, 3. that she may not respect persons; *stopping the left ear*, 4. 146 to be reserved for the other party

In viâ pergit
cautè (providè)
ne impingat
aut aberret.

Sedulitas, 1. am-
at labores,
fugit Ignaviam,
semper est in
opere,
ut Formica, 2.
& comportat,
ut illa, sibi,
omnium rerum
Copiam, 3.

Non semper
dormit, ferias ag-
it,
aut ut Ignavus, 4.
& Cicada, 5.
quos Inopia, 6.
tandem premit.

Urget incepta
alacriter
ad finem usque;
procrastinat ni-
hil,
nec cantat
cantilenam
Corvi, 7.
qui ingeminat
Cras, Cras.

which saith over
and over,
140 Cras, Cras.
After labours
undergone, and
ended,
being even wea-
ried,
she resteth her self;
but being refreshed
with Rest,
that she may not
use her self
to Idleness, she fal-
leth again
to her Business,
A diligent Scholar
is like Bees, 8.
which carry honey
from divers Flow-
ers, 9.
into their Hive, 10.

Post labores
exantlatos,
& lassata,
quiescit;
sed recreata Qui-
ete,
ne adsuescat
Otio, redit
ad Negotia.

Diligens Discip-
ulus,
similis est
Apibus, 8.
qui congerunt
mel
ex variis
Floribus, 9.
in Alveare suum,
10.

CXII.

Temperance.
Temperantia.

Temperance, 1.
prescribeth a mean
to meat and drink, 2.
and restraineth the
desire,
as with a Bridle, 3.
141 and so moder-
ateth all things,
lest any thing
too much be done.

Revellers

Temperantia,
1.
præscribit
modum
Cibo & Potui,
2.
& continet cu-
pidinem,
ceu Freno, 3.
& sic moder-
atur omnia
ne quid
nimis fiat.

Heluones (ga-

are made drunk, 4.
they stumble, 5.
they spue, 6.
and babble, 7.*

From Drunkenness
proceedeth Lasciv-
iousness;
from this a lewd Life
amongst Whoremas-
ters, 8.
and Whores, 9.
in kissing,
touching,
embracing,
and dancing, 10.

CXIII.

Fortitude.
Fortitudo.

Fortitude, 1.
is undaunted in
adversity,
142 and bold as a
Lion, 2. but
not haughty in
Prosperity,
leaning on her
own Pillar, 3.
Constancy, and
being the same in
all things,
ready to undergo
both
estates with an
even mind.
She receiveth the
strokes
of Misfortune
with the Shield, 4.

neones)
inebriantur, 4.
titubant, 5.
ructant (vo-
munt), 6.
& rixantur, 7.

E Crapula
oritur Las-
civia;
ex hâc Vita li-
bidinosa
inter Fornica-
tores, 8.
& Scorta, 9.
osculando
(basiando),
palpando,
amplexando,
& tripudiando,
10.

Fortitudo, 1.
impavida est in
adversis,
& confidens ut
Leo, 2. at
non tumida in Se-
cundis,
innixa suo Colu-
mini, 3.
Constantiæ; &
eadem in om-
nibus,
parata ad feren-
dam utramque
fortunam æquo
animo.
Excipit ictus
Infortunii
Clypeo, 4.
Tolerantiæ: &

Poland, 18.
The Netherlands, 19.
Denmark, 20.
Norway, 21.
Swethland, 22.
Lapland, 23.
Finland, 24.
Lisland, 25.
Prussia, 26.
Muscovy, 27.
and Russia, 28.

Lituania, 17.
Polonia 18.
Belgium, 19.
Dania, 20.
Norvegia, 21.
Suecia, 22.
Lappia, 23.
Finnia, 24.
Livonia 25.
Borussia, 26.
Muscovia, 27.
Russia, 28.

CIX.

Moral Philosophy.

Ethica.

This *Life* is a *way*,
or a *place divided into two ways*,
like *Pythagoras's Letter* Y.
broad, 1.
on the left hand track;
narrow, 2. on the right;
that belongs to *Vice*, 3.
this to *Vertue*, 4.
Mind, Young Man, 5.
imitate *Hercules*:
leave the left hand way,
turn from Vice;
the *Entrance*, 6. is fair,
but the *End*, 7.
is ugly and steep down.
Go on the right hand,
though it be thorny, 8.
no way is unpassible
to vertue; follow whither
vertue leadeth
through narrow places
to stately palaces,
to the Tower of honour, 9.
Keep the middle and streight *path*,
and thou shalt go very safe.
Take heed thou do not go
too much on the right hand, 10.
Bridle in, 12.
the wild Horse, 11.
of Affection,
lest thou fall down headlong.
See thou dost not go amiss on the
left hand, 13.
in an ass-like sluggishness, 14.
but go onwards constantly,
persevere to the end,
and thou shalt be crown'd, 15.

Vita hæc est *via*,
sive *bivium*,
simile
Litteræ *Pithagoricæ* Y.
latum, 1.
sinistro tramite angustum, 2.
dextro;
ille *Vitii*, 3.
est his *Virtutis*, 4.
Adverte juvenis, 5.
imitare *Herculem*;
linque sinistram,
aversare Vitium;
Aditus speciosus, 6.
sed *Exitus*, 7.
turpis & præceps
Dextera ingredere,
utut spinosa, 8.
nulla via invia virtuti; sequere quâ
viâ ducit virtus
per *angusta*,
ad *augusta*,
ad *Arcem honoris*, 9.

Tene medium & rectum *tramitem*;
ibis tutissimus.
Cave excedas ad dextram, 10.

Compesce freno, 12.
equum ferocem, 11. Affectûs
ne præceps fias.
Cave deficias ad sinistram, 13.
segnitie asininâ, 14.
sed progredere constanter
pertende ad finem,
& coronaberis, 15.

CX.

Prudence.

Prudentia.

Prudence, 1.
looketh upon all things
as a *Serpent*, 2.

Prudentia, 1.
circumspectat omnia
ut *Serpens*, 2.

and doeth,
speaketh, or
thinketh nothing vain.
She *looks backwards*, 3.
as into a *Looking glass*, 4.
to *things past*,
and seeth *before her*, 5.
as with a *Perspective-glass*, 7.
things to come,
or the *End*, 6.
and so she perceiveth
what she hath done
and
what remaineth to be done.
She proposeth
an *Honest, Profitable*
and withal, if it may be done,
a *Pleasant End*,
to her Actions.*

Having foreseen *End*,
she looketh out *Means*,
as a *Way*, 8.
which leadeth to End;
but such as are certain
and easie, and fewer
rather than more,
lest anything should hinder.
She watcheth *Opportunity*, 9.
(which having
a *bushy fore-head* 10.
and being *bald-pated*, 11.
and moreover
having *wings*, 12.
doth quickly slip away,)

& Terram, 3.
obtegit illum
umbrâ suâ;
& hoc vocamus
Eclipsin Solis,
quia adimit nobis
prospectum Solis,
& lucem ejus;
nec tamen Sol
patitur aliquid,
sed Terra.

They measure Longitude
of it by *Climates*, 1.
and the *Latitude*
by *Parallels*, 2.

The *Ocean*, 3.
compasseth it about,
and five *Seas* wash it,
the *Mediterranean Sea*, 4.
the *Baltick Sea*, 5.
the *Red Sea*, 6.
the *Persian Sea*, 7.
and the *Caspian Sea*, 8.

cujus *Centrum* est.
Longitudinem ejus
dimetiuntur *Climatibus*, 1.
Latitudinem,
lineis *Parallelis*, 2.

Oceanus, 3.
ambit eam
& *Maria* V.
perfundunt
Mediterraneum, 4.
Balticum, 5.
Erythræum, 6.
Persicum, 7.
Caspium, 8.

which
is subdivided into
Europe, 13.
Asia, 14. *Africa*, 15.
America, 16.16.
(whose Inhabitants are
Antipodes to us;)
and the *South Land*, 17.17.
yet unknown.
They that dwell
under the *North pole*, 18.
have the days and nights
6 months long.
Infinite *Islands*
float in the Seas.

Europam, 13.
Asiam, 14. &
Africam, 15.
in *Americam*, 16. 16.
(cujus incolæ sunt
Antipodes nobis;)
& in *Terram Australem*, 17.17.
adhuc incognitam.

Habitantes
sub *Arcto*, 18.
habent Dies
Noctes
semestrales,

Infinitæ *Insulæ*
natant in maribus.

CVII. b

The terrestial Sphere.

Sphera terrestris.

CVIII.

Europe.

Europa.

Terra est rotunda,
fingenda igitur
duobus *Hemisphæriis*, a.b.

Ambitus ejus
est *graduum*
CCCLX.
(quorum
quisque facit
LX. Milliaria
Anglica
vel 21600 Milliarium)
& tamen est
punctum,
collata cum
orbe,

It is divided into
V. *Zones*,
whereof the II.
frigid ones,
9.9.
134 are uninhabitable;
the II. *Temperate*
ones, 10.10.
and the *Torrid*
one, 11.
habitable.

Besides it is divided
into three *Continents*;
this of ours, 12.

Distribuitur in
Zonas V.,
quarum duæ
frigidæ,
9.9.
sunt inhabitabiles;
duæ *Temperatæ*,
10.10.
& *Torrida*, 11.
habitantur.

Ceterum divisa est
in tres *Continentes*;
nostram, 12. quæ
subdividitur in

The chief *Kingdoms*
of *Europe*, are
135 *Spain*, 1.
France, 2.
Italy, 3.
England, 4.
Scotland, 5.
Ireland, 6.
Germany, 7.
Bohemia, 8.
Hungary, 9.
Croatia, 10.
Dacia, 11.
Sclavonia, 12.
Greece, 13.
Thrace, 14.
Podolia, 15.
Tartary, 16.
Lituania, 17.

In *Europâ* nostrâ
sunt *Regna* primaria,
Hispania, 1.
Gallia, 2.
Italia, 3.
Anglia (Britania), 4.
Scotia, 5.
Hibernia, 6.
Germania, 7.
Bohemia, 8.
Hungaria, 9.
Croatia, 10.
Dacia, 11.
Sclavonia, 12.
Græcia, 13.
Thracia, 14.
Podolia, 15.
Tartaria, 16.

Capricorn, 13.
and the two
Polar Circles, 14.
15.
129

& duo
Polares, 14.15.

in Opposition,
☉ and ♄ in a Trine Aspect,
☉ and ♃ in a Quartile,
☉ and ♀ in a Sextile.

☉ and Luna
in Oppositione,
☉ & ♄ in Trigono,
☉ & ♃ in Quadratura,
☉ & ♀ in Sextili.

)
Otherwise it waxeth, 2.4.
or waneth, 6.8
and is said to be horned,
or more than half round.

CIV.

The Aspects of the Planets.

Planetarum Aspectus.

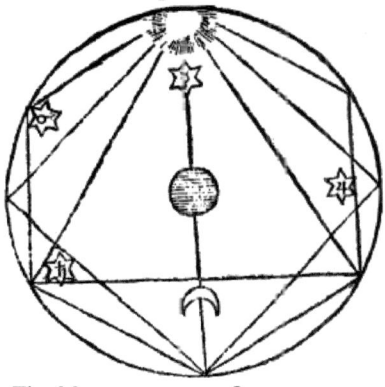

The *Moon*
runneth through the *Zodiack*
every *Month*.

The *Sun*, ☉ in a *Year*.

Mercury, ☿
and *Venus*, ♀
about the Sun,
the one in a hundred and fifteen,
the other in 585 days.

Mars, ♂ in two years;

Jupiter, ♃
in almost twelve;

Saturn, ♄
in thirty years.

Hereupon they meet variously among themselves,
and have mutual Aspects
one towards another.

130 As here the ☉
and ☿ are
in *Conjunction*.
☉ and *Moon*

Luna
percurrit Zodiacum
singulis Mensibus.

Sol, ☉ Anno.

Mercurius, ☿
& *Venus*, ♀
circa Solem,
illa CXV.,
hæc
DLXXXV.
Diebus.

Mars, ♂ Biennio;

Jupiter, ♃
ferè duodecim;

Saturnus, ♄
triginta annis.

Hinc conveniunt
variè inter se
& se mutuo adspiciunt.

Ut hic sunt, ☉
& ☿
in *Conjunctione*,

CV.

The Apparitions of the Moon.

Phases Lunæ.

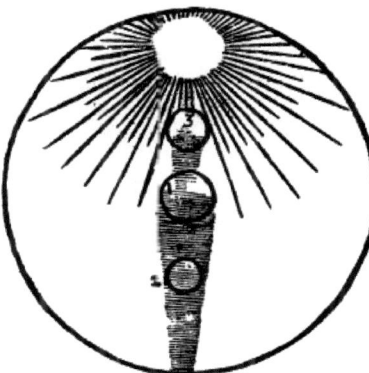

The *Moon* shineth not by her own *Light*
but that which is borrowed of the *Sun*.

For the one half of it
is always enlightned,
the other remaneth darkish.

Hereupon we see it in
Conjunction with the *Sun*, 1.
to be obscure, almost none at all;
in *Opposition*, 5.
131 whole and clear,
(and we call it the *Full Moon*;)
sometimes in the half,
(and we call it the *Prime*, 3.
and last *Quarter*, 7.

Luna, lucet
non sua propria *Luce*,
sed mutuatâ a *Sole*.

Nam altera ejus medietas
semper illuminatur,
altera manet caliginosa.

Hinc videmus, in *Conjunctione Solis*, 1.
obscuram, imo nullam:
in *Oppositione*, 5.
totam & lucidam,
(& vocamus *Plenilunium*;)
alias dimidiam,
(& dicimus *Primam*, 3.
& ultimam *Quadram*, 7.)

CVI.

The Eclipses.

Eclipses.

The *Sun*
is the fountain of light,
inlightning all things,
but the *Earth*, 1.
and the *Moon*, 2.
being shady bodies,
are not pierced with its rays,
for they cast a shadow
upon the place just over against them.

Therefore, when the Moon lighteth
132 into the shadow
of the *Earth* 2.
it is darkened, which we call an *Eclipse*,
or defect.

But when the Moon

CIV.

The Celestial Sphere.

Sphera cælestis.

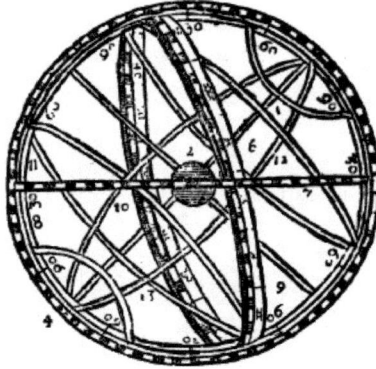

Astronomy considereth the *motion of the Stars*, Astrology the Effects of them.

The *Globe of Heaven* is turned about upon an *Axle-tree*, 1. about the *Globe of the Earth*, 2. in the space of XXIV. hours.

The *Pole-stars*, or *Pole*, the *Arctick*, 3. the *Antarctick*, 4. conclude the *Axle-tree* at both ends.

The *Heaven* is full of Stars every where.

There are reckoned above a *thousand fixed Stars*; but of *Constellations* towards the *North*, XXI. towards the *South*, XVI.

Add to these the XII. *signs* of the *Zodiaque*, 5. every one XXX. degrees, whose names are ♈ *Aries* ♉ *Taurus*, ♊ *Gemini*, ♋ *Cancer*, ♌ *Leo*, ♍ *Virgo*, ♎ *Libra*, ♏ *Scorpius*, ♐ *Sagittarius*, ♑ *Capricorn*, ♒ *Aquarius*, ♓ *Pisces*.

Under this move the seven *Wandring-stars* which they call *Planets*, whose way is a circle in the middle of the Zodiack, called the *Ecliptick*, 6.

Other Circles are the *Horizon*, 7. the *Meridian*, 8. the *Æquator*, 9. the two *Colures*, the one of the *Equinocts*, 10. (of the *Spring* when the ☉ entreth into ♈; *Autumnal* when it entreth in ♎) the other of the *Solstices*, 11. (of the *Summer*, when the ☉ entreth into ♋; of the *Winter* when it entreth into ♑) the *Tropicks*, the *Tropick of Cancer*, 12. the *Tropick of*

Astronomia considerat motus Astrorum, Astrologia eorum Effectus.

Globus Cœli volvitur super Axem, 1. circa globum terræ, 2. spacio XXIV. horarum.

Stellæ polares, Arcticus, 3. Antarcticus, 4. finiunt Axem utrinque.

Cœlum est Stellatum undique.

Stellarum fixarum numerantur plus mille; Siderum verò Septentrionarium, XXI. Meridionalium, XVI.

Adde *Signa*, XII. *Zodiaci*, 5. quodlibet graduum, XXX, quorum nomina sunt ♈ *Aries* ♉ *Taurus*, ♊ *Gemini*, ♋ *Cancer*, ♌ *Leo*, ♍ *Virgo*, ♎ *Libra*, ♏ *Scorpius*, ♐ *Sagittarius*, ♑ *Capricorn*, ♒ *Aquarius*, ♓ *Pisces*.

Sub hoc cursitant Stellæ errantes VII. quas vocant *Planetas*, quorum via est *Circulvs*, in medio Zodiaci, dictus *Ecliptica*, 6.

Alii Circuli sunt Horizon, 7. Meridianus, 8. Equator, 9. duo Coluri, alter Æquinoxiorum, 10. (Verni, quando ☉ ingreditur ♈; Autumnalis, quando ingreditur ♎) alter Solsticiorum, 11. (Æstivi, quando ☉ ingreditur ♋; Hyberni, quando ingreditur ♑) duo Tropici, Tr. Cancri, 12. Tr. Capricorni, 13.

Palimocesto, *el Calculis*, 4. *uper Abacum*.

Rustici numerant, *Decussibus*, & *Quincunibus*, per *Duodenas*, *Quindenas*, & *Sexagenas*.

Geometra metitur Altitudinem Turris, 1.2. aut distantiam Locorum, 3.4. sive Quadrante, 5. sive Radio, 6. Designat Figuras rerum Lineis, 7. Angulis, 8. & Circulis, 9. ad Regulam, 10. Normam, 11. & Circinum, 12. Ex his oriuntur Cylindrus, 13. Trigonus 14. Tetragonus, 15. & aliæ figuræ.

Apothegms, Sentences, Similies, Hierogylphicks, &c.	bia) Apothegmata, Sententiæ (Gnomæ) Similia, Hieroglyphica, &c.
Poetry, 9. gathereth these Flowers of Speech, 10. and tieth them as it were into a little Garland, 11. and so making of Prose a Poem, it maketh several sorts of Verses and Odes, and is therefore crowned with a Laurel, 12.	Poesis, 9. colligit hos Flores Orationis, 10. & colligat quasi in Corallam, 11. atque ita, faciens è prosa ligatam orationem, componit varia Carmina & Hymnos (Odas) ac propterea coronatur Lauru, 12.
Musick, 13. setteth Tunes, 14. with pricks, to which it setteth words, and so singeth alone, or in Consort, or by Voice, or Musical Instruments, 15.	Musica, 13. componit Melodias, 14. Notis, quibus aptat verba, atque ita cantat sola vel Concentu (Symphonia), aut voce aut Instrumentis Musicis, 15.

CI.

Musical Instruments.

Instrumenta musica.

Musical Instruments are	Musica instrumenta sunt
those which make a sound: First, when they are beaten upon, as a Cymbal, 1. with a Pestil, a little Bell, 2. with an Iron pellet within; or Rattle, 3. by tossing it about: a Jews-Trump, 4. being put to the mouth, with the fingers; a Drum, 5. and a Kettle, 6 with a Drumstick, 7. as also the Dulcimer, 8. with the Shepherds-harp, 9. and the Tymbrel, 10. Secondly, upon which strings are stretched, and struck upon, as the Psalter, 11. 124 and the Virginals, 12. with both hands; the Lute, 13. (in which is the Neck, 14. the Belly, 15. the Pegs, 16. by which the Strings, 17. are stretched upon the Bridge, 18.) the Cittern, 19. with the right hand only, the Vial, 20. with a Bow, 21. and the Harp, 23. with a Wheel within,	quæ edunt vocem: Primò, cum pulsantur, ut Cymbalum, 1. Pistillo, Tintinnabulum, 2. intus Globulo ferreo, Crepitaculum, 3. circumversando; Crembalum, 4. ori admotum, Digito; Tympanum, 5. & Ahenum, 6. Claviculâ, 7. ut & Sambuca, 8. cum Organo pastoritio, 9. & Sistrum (Crotalum), 10. Secundò, in quibus Chordæ intenduntur & plectuntur ut Nablium, 11. cum Clavircordio, 12. utrâque manu; Testudo (Chelys), 13. (in quâ Jugum, 14. Magadium, 15. & Verticilli, 16. quibus Nervi, 17. intenduntur super Ponticulam, 18.) & Cythara, 19. Dexterâ tantum, Pandura, 20. Plectro, 21. & Lyra, 23. intus rotâ, quæ versatur: Dimensiones, 22. in singulis tanguntur	which is turned about: the Stops, 22. in every one are touched with the left hand At last, those which are blown, as with the mouth the Flute, 24. the Shawm, 25. the Bag-pipe, 26. the Cornet, 27. the Trumpet, 28, 29. or with Bellows, as a pair of Organs, 30.

CII.

Philosophy.

Philosophia.

The Naturalist, 1 vieweth all the works of God in the World. The Supernaturalist, 2. searches out the Causes and Effects of things The Arithmetician, reckoneth numbers, by adding, subtracting, multiplying and dividing, and that either by

aliquando
Columnis, 11.
divisa cumq;
*Notis Marginal-
ibus*, 12.

120 these are
chastised
with a *Ferrula*,
11.
and a *Rod*, 12.

Ferulâ (baculo),
11.
& *Virgâ*, 12.

XCIX.

The Study.

Museum.

chola, 1.
st *Officina*, in
uâ
ovelli Animi for-
antur
 virtutem, &
stinguitur in
lasses.

ræceptor, 2.
det in *Cathedra*,

iscipuli, 4.
Subselliis, 5.
e docet, hi dis-
nt.

uædam
æscribuntur illis
retâ in *Tabella*,

uidam sedent
 Mensam, &
ribunt, 7.
se corrigit Men-
s, 8.

uidam stant, &
citant
andata
emoriæ, 9.

uidam confabu-
ntur, 10.
gerunt se
tulantes, & neg-
entes;
castigantur

The *Study*, 1.
is a place where a
Student, 2.
apart from Men,
sitteth alone,
addicted to his
Studies,
whilst he readeth
Books, 3.
which being within
his reach
he layeth open up-
on a *Desk*, 4.
and picketh all the
best things
out of them
into his own *Man-
ual*, 5.
or marketh them in
them
with a *Dash*, 6.
or a *little Star*, 7.
in the *Margent*.

Being to sit up late,
121 he setteth a
Candle, 8.
on a *Candlestick*,
9.
which is snuffed
with *Snuffers*, 10.
before the Candle,
he placeth a
Screen, 11.
which is green, that
it may not

Museum, 1.
est locus ubi *Stu-
diosus*, 2.
secretus ab *Ho-
minibus*,
sedet solus
deditus *Studiis*,
dum lectitat *Li-
bros*, 3.
quos penes se
& exponit super
Pluteum, 4.
& excerpit opti-
ma quæque
ex illis
in *Manuale* su-
um, 5.
notat in illis
Liturâ, 6.
vel *Asterisco*, 7.
ad *Margiem*.

Lucubraturus,
elevat *Lychnum*
(*Canelam*), 8.
in *Candelabra*,
9.
qui emungitur
Emunctorio, 10.
ante Lynchum
collocat *Um-
braculum*, 11.
quod viride est,
ne

hurt his eye-sight;
richer Persons use
a *Taper*,
for a *Tallow-candle*
stinketh and
smoaketh.

A *Letter*, 12. is
wrapped up,
writ upon, 13.
and sealed, 14.

Going abroad by
night,
he maketh use of a
Lanthorn, 15.
or a *Torch*, 16.

hebetet oculo-
rum aciem;
opulentiores
utuntur *Cereo*
nam *Candela se-
bacea*
fœtet & fumigat.

Epistola, 12.
complicatur,
inscribitur, 13.
& obsignatur,
14.

Prodiens noctu
utitur *Lanterna*,
15.
vel *Face*, 16.

C.

Arts belonging to Speech.

Artes Sermones.

Grammar, 1.
122 is conversant
about *Letters*, 2.
of which it maketh
Words, 3.
and teacheth how
to utter, write, 4.
put together and
part
them rightly.

Grammatica, 1.
versatur circa
Literas, 2.
ex quibus com-
ponit
Voces, verba, 3.
docetque
eloqui, scribere,
4.
construere, dis-
tinguere
(interpungere)
eas recte.

Rhetorick, 5.
doth as it were
paint, 6.
a rude form, 7.
of Speech
with *Oratory
Flourishes*, 8.
such as are *Figures,
Elegancies,
Adagies*,

Rhetorica, 5.
pingit, 6.
quasi rudem *for-
mam*, 7.
*Sermonis
Oratoriis Pig-
mentis*, 8.
ut sunt *Figuræ,
Elegantiæ,
Adagia* (prover-

Visorum, 2.)
composeth words
in a *Composing-
stick*, 3.
till a *Line* be
made;
he putteth these in
a *Gally*, 4.
till a *Page*, 6. be
made,
and these again
in a *Form*, 7.
and he locketh
them up
in *Iron Chases*, 8.
with *Coyns*, 9.
lest they should
drop out,
and putteth them
under
the *Press*, 10.
Then the *Press-
man*
beateth it over
with *Printers Ink*,
by means of
Balls, 11.
spreadeth upon it
the Papers
put in the *Frisket*,
12.
which being put
under
the *Spindle*, 14.
on the *Coffin*, 13.
and pressed down
with
a *Bar*, 15. he
maketh
to take impres-
sion.
116

componit Verba
Gnomone, 3.
donec versus fiat;
hos indit *Formæ*,
4.
donec *Pagina*, 6.
fiat;
has iterum
*Tabulâ composi-
toriâ*, 7.
coarctaque eos
*Marginibus fer-
reis*, 8.
ope *Cochlearum*,
9.
ne dilabantur,
ac subjicit
Prelo, 10.

Tum *Impressor*
illinit
*Atramento im-
pressorio*
ope *Pilarum*, 11.
super imponit
Chartas
inditas *Operculo*,
12.
quas subditas
Trochleæ, 14.
in *Tigello*, 13.
& impressas
Suculâ 15. facit
imbibere typos.

XCV.

The Booksellers Shop.

Bibliopolium.

The *Bookseller*, 1
selleth *Books*
in a *Booksellers
Shop*, 2.
of which he
writeth
a *Catalogue*, 3.
The Books are

Bibliopola, 1.
vendit *Libros*
in *Bibliopolio*, 2.
quorum conscrib-
it
Catalogum, 3.

Libri disponuntur

placed
on *Shelves*, 4.
and are laid open
for use
upon a *Desk*, 5.
A Multitude of
Books
is called a *Library*,
6.
117

per *Repositoria*,
4.
& exponuntur ad
usum,
super *Pluteum*, 5.
Multitudo Libro-
rum
vocatur *Biblio-
theca*, 6.

XCVI.

The Book-binder.

Bibliopegus.

In times past they
glewed
Paper to Paper,
and rolled them
up together
into one *Roll*, 1.

At this day
the *Book-binder*
bindeth Books,
whilst he wipeth,
2. over
Papers steept
in *Gum-water*,
and then
foldeth them to-
gether, 3.
beateth with a
hammer, 4.
then stitcheth
them up, 5.

Olim agglutina-
bant
Chartam Chartæ,
convolvebantque
eas
in unum *Volumen*,
1.

Hodiè
Compactor
compingit Libros,
dum tergit, 2.
chartas maceratas
aquâ glutinosâ,
deinde
complicat, 3.
malleat, 4.
tum consuit, 5.
conprimit
Prelo, 6.
quod habet duos
Cochleas, 7.

presseth them
in a *Press*, 6.
which hath two
Screws, 7.
glueth them on the
back,
cutteth off the
edges
with a *round
Knife*, 8.
and at last cov-
ereth them
with *Parchment* or
Leather, 9.
maketh them
handsome,
and setteth on
Clasps, 10.
118

XCVII.

A Book.

Liber.

A *Book*
as to its outward
shape,
is either in *Folio*, 1.
or in *Quarto*, 2.
in *Octavo*, 3.
in *Duodecimo*, 4.
either made to op
Side-wise, 5.
or *Long-wise*, 6.
with *Brazen Clasps*,
7.
or *Strings*, 8.
and *Square-bofles*
9.

Within are *Leaves*,
10.
with two *Pages*,

adjuvat.
Quidam evadunt,
vel *tabula*, 7.
ac enatando,
vel *Scapha*, 8.

Pars Mercium
cum mortuis
a *Mari*, 9.
in littora defertur.

Veteres scribebant
in *Tabellis ceratis*
æneo *Stilo*, 1.
ujus *parte cuspi-
ata*, 2.
xarabantur
literæ,
ursum vero oblit-
rabantur
lanâ.

Deinde
literas pingebant
ubtili *Calamo*, 4.
Jos utimur *Anse-
ina Penna*, 5.
ujus *Caulem*, 6.
emperamus
calpello, 7.
Im intingimus
renam
Atramentario,

uod obstruitur

which is stopped
with a *Stopple*, 9.
and we put our
Pens,
into a *Pennar*, 10.
We dry a Writing
113 with *Blot-
ting-paper*,
or *Calis-sand*
out of a *Sand-
box*, 11.

And we indeed
write from the left
hand
towards the right,
12.
the *Hebrews*
from the right
hand
towards the left,
13.
the *Chinese* and
other *Indians*,
from the top
downwards, 14.

XCIII.
Paper.

Papyrus.

The Ancients used
Beech-Boards, 1.
or *Leaves*, 2.
as also *Barks*, 3.
of *Trees*;
especially of an
Egyptian Shrub,
which was called
Papyrus.

Now *Paper* is in
use
which the *Paper-
maker*

Operculo, 9.
& *Pennas*
recondimus in
Calamario, 10.
Siccamus Scriptu-
ram
Chartâ bibulâ,
vel *Arenâ scripto-
ria*,
ex *Theca Pulver-
aria*, 11.

Et nos quidem
scribimus â sinis-
tra
dextrorsum, 12.
Hebræi
â dextrâ
sinistrorsum, 13.
Chinenses & *Indi*
alii,
â summo
deorsum, 14.

Veteres utebantur
Tabulis Faginis,
1.
aut *Foliis*, 2.
ut & *Libris*, 3. *Ar-
borum*;
præsertim Arbus-
culæ Ægyptiæ,
cui nomen erat
Papyrus.

Nunc *Charta* est
in usu,
quam *Chattopœus*
in *mola Pa-*

114 maketh in a
Paper-mill, 4.
of *Linen rags*, 5.
stamped to *Mash*,
6.
which being taken
up
in *Frames*, 7.
he spreadeth into
Sheets, 8.
and setteth them
in the Air
that they may be
dryed.
Twenty-five of
these
make a *Quire*, 9.
twenty Quires a
Ream, 10.
and ten of these
a *Bale of Paper*,
11.
That which is to
last long
is written on
Parchment, 12.

XCIV.
Printing.

Typographia.

The *Printer* hath
metal *Letters*
in a large number
put into *Boxes*, 5.

The *Compositor*,
1.
115 taketh them
out one by one
and according to
the *Copy*,
(which he hath
fastened
before him in a

pyracea, 4. con-
ficit
è *Linteis vetustis*,
5.
in *Pulmentum*
contusis, 6.
quod haustum
Normulis, 7.
diducit in *Plagu-
las*, 8.
exponitque aëri,
ut siccentur.

Harum XXV.
faciunt *Scapum*,
9.
XX. Scapi *Volu-
men minus*, 10.
horum X.
Volumen majus,
11.

Duraturum diu
scribitur in
Membrana, 12.

Typographus ha-
bet
Typos Metallos,
magno numero
distributos per
Loculamenta, 5.

Typotheta, 1.
eximit illos singu-
latim,
& secundum *ex-
emplar*,
(quod habet præ-
fixum
sibi *Retinaculo*, 2.
)

learned
to tread the water, 4.
being plunged
up to the girdle-
stead,
and carrying
their Cloaths upon
their head.

A *Diver*, 5.
can swim also un-
der
the water like a
Fish.

didicerunt
calcare aquam, 4.
immersi
cingulo tenus
& gestantes
Vestes supra ca-
put.

Urinator, 5.
etiam natare
potest sub
aquâ, ut Piscis.

LXXXIX.

A Galley.

Navis actuaria.

A *Ship* furnished
with *Oars*, 1.
is a *Barge*, 2.
or a *Foyst*, &c.
in which the *Row-
ers*, 3.
109 sitting on
Seats, 4.
by the *Oar-rings*,
row, by striking
the water
with the *Oars*, 5.
The *Ship-master*, 6.
standing in the
Fore-castle,
and the *Steers-
man*, 7.
sitting at the
Stern,
and holding the
Rudder, 8.
steer the *Vessel*.

Navis instructa
Remis, 1.
est Uniremis, 2.
vel Biremis, &c.
in quâ Remiges, 3.
considentes pre
Transtra, 4.
ad Scalmos,
remigant pellendo
aquam
Remis,

Proreta, 6.
stans in Prora,
& Gubernator, 7.
sedens in Puppi,
tensque
Clavum, 8.
gubernant
Navigium.

XC.

A Merchant-ship.

Navis oneraria.

A *Ship*, 1.
is driven onward
not by Oars, but by
the only
force of the Winds.
In it is a *Mast*, 2. set
up,
fastened with
Shrouds, 3.
on all sides to
the *main-chains*.
110 to which the
Sail-yards, 4.
are tied,
and the *Sails*, 5. to
these,
which are *spread
open*, 6.
to the wind,
and are hoysed by
Bowlings, 7.
The Sails are
the *Main-sail*, 8.
the *Trinket*, or *Fore-
sail*, 9.
the *Misen-sail* or
Poop-sail, 10.
The *Beak*, 11.
is in the *Fore-deck*.
The *Ancient*, 12.
is placed in the
Stern.

On the Mast
is the *Foretop*, 13.
the *Watch-tower* of
the Ship
and over the *Fore-
top*
a *Vane*, 14.

Navigium, 1.
impellitur,
non remis, sed
solâ
vi Ventorum.
In illo Malus, 2.
erigitur,
firmatus Fu-
nibus, 3.
undique ad
Oras Navis,
cui annectuntur
Antennæ, 4.
his, Vela, 5.
quæ expandun-
tur, 6.
ad Ventum
& Versoriis, 7.
versantur.

Vela sunt
Artemon, 8.
Dolon, 9.
& Epidromus, 10.

Rostrum, 11.
est in Prora.
Signum (vexil-
lum), 12.
ponitur in Pup-
pi.

In Malo
est Corbis, 13.
Specula Navis
& supra
Galeam
Aplustre, 14.
Ventorum In-

to shew which way
the Wind standeth
The ship is stayed
with an *Anchor*,
The depth is fath-
omed
with a *Plummet*,
Passengers walk
and down
the *Decks*, 17
The Sea men run
and fro
through the *Hatch-
es*, 18.
And thus, even S
are passed over.

111

XCI.

Ship-wreck.

Naufragium.

When a *Storm*, 1
ariseth on a sud-
den,
they strike *Sail*, 2
lest the Ship
should be
dashed against
Rocks, 3 or
light upon
Shelves, 4.
If they cannot hin-
der her
they suffer *Ship-
wreck*, 5.
And then the men
the *Wares*, and al
things
are miserably los
Nor doth the
Sheat-anchor, 6.
being cast with a
Cable,

unt
duodecim
Radii, 15.
Orbile ambit
hos, compositum
è sex *Absidibus*, 16.
& totidem *Canthis*, 17.
Corbes &
Crates, 18.
imponuntur
Currui.

pot, 9.
and stoppeth the
wheel
with a *Trigen*, 10.
106 in a steep descent.
And thus the
Coach is driven
along the *Wheel-
ruts*, 11.
Great Persons are
carryed
with six Horses,
12.
by two *Coachmen*,
in a Hanging-wagon,
which is called
a *Coach*, 13.
Others *with two
Horses*, 14.
in a *Chariot*, 15.
Horse Litters, 16,
17.
are carried by two
Horses.
They use
Pack-Horses,
instead of *Waggons*,
thorow *Hills*
that are not passable, 18.

Sufflamine, 10.
in præcipiti descensu.

Et sic aurigatur
per *Orbitas*, 11.

Magnates vehuntur
Sejugibus, 12.
duobus *Rhedariis*,
Curru pensili,
qui vocatur
Carpentum (Pilentum), 13.
Alii *Bijugibus*,
14.
Essedo, 15.
Arceræ, 16. &
Lacticæ, 17.
portantur à
duobus Equis.
Utuntur
Jumentis Clitellariis,
loco *Curruum*,
per *montes
invios*, 18.

LXXXVII.

Passing over Waters.

Transitus Aquarum.

Lest he that is to
pass
over a River
should be wet,
107 *Bridges*, 1.
were invented for
Carriages,

Trajecturus
flumen ne madefiat,
Pontes, 1.
excogitati sunt
pro Vehiculis
& *Ponticuli*, 2.

and *Foot-bridges*,
2.
for Foot-men.
If a river
have a *Foord*, 3.
it is *waded over*,
4.
Flotes, 5. also are
made
of Timber pinned
together;
or *Ferry-boats*, 6.
of planks laid
close together
for fear they
should
receive Water.
Besides *Scullers*,
7.
are made, which
are rowed with an
Oar, 8.
or *Pole*, 9.
or haled with
an *Haling-rope*,
10.

pro Peditibus.

Si Flumen
habet *Vadum*, 3.
vadatur, 4.

Rates, 5. etiam
struuntur
ex compactis tignis:
vel *Pontones*, 6.
ex trabibus consolidatis,
ne excipiant
aquam.

Porrò *Lintres*
(Lembi), 7.
fabricantur, qui
aguntur *Remo*, 8.
vel *Conto*, 9.
aut trahuntur
Remulco, 10.

LXXXVIII.

Swimming.

Natatus.

Men are wont also
to swim over Waters
108 upon a *bundle
of flags*, 1.
and besides upon
blown
Beast-bladders, 2.
and after, by
throwing
their *Hands* and
Feet, 3.
abroad.
And at last they

Solent etiam
tranare aquas
super *scirpeum
fascem*, 1.
porrò super inflatas
boum Vesicas, 2.
deinde liberè
jactatu
Manuum Pedumque, 3.

Tandem

beareth on his shoulders	portat humeris
101 in a *Budget*, 2.	in *Bulga*, 2.
those things which his *Satchel*, 3. or *Pouch*, 4. cannot hold.	quæ non capit *Funda*, 3. vel *Marsupium*, 4.
He is covered with a *Cloak*, 5.	Tegitur *Lacernâ*, 5.
He holdeth a *Staff*, 6. in his hand wherewith to bear up himself.	Tenet *Baculum*, 6. Manu quo se fulciat.
He hath need of *Provision for the way*, as also of a pleasant and merry *Companion*, 7.	Opus habet *Viatico*, ut & fido & facundo *Comite*, 7.
Let him not forsake the *High-road*, 9. for a *Foot-way*, 8. unless it be a *beaten Path*.	Non deserat *Viam regiam* propter *Semitam*, 8. nisi sit *Callis tritus*.
By-ways, 10. and *places where two ways meet*, 11. deceive and lead men aside into *uneven-places*, 12. so do not *By-paths*, 13. and *Cross-ways*, 14.	*Avia*, 10. & *Bivia*, 11. fallunt & seducunt, in *Salebras*, 12 non æquè *Tramites*, 13. & *Compita*, 14.
Let him therefore enquire of *those he meeteth*, 15. which way he must go; and let him take heed of *Robbers*, 16. as in the *way*, so also in the *Inn*, 17. where he lodgeth all Night.	Sciscitet igitur *obvios*, 15. quâ sit eundum; & caveat *Prædones*, 16 ut in viâ, sic etiam in *Diversorio*, 17. ubi pernoctat.

102

LXXXIV.

The Horse-man.

Eques.

The *Horse-man*, 1.	*Eques*, 1.
setteth a *Saddle*, 2. on his *Horse*, 3. and girdeth it on with a *Girth*, 4.	imponit *Equo*, 2. *Ephippium*, 3. idque succingit *Cingulo*, 4.
He layeth a *Saddle-cloth*, 5. also upon him.	Insternit etiam *Dorsuale*, 5.
He decketh him with *Trappings*, a *Forestall*, 6. a *Breast-cloth*, 7. and a *Crupper*, 8.	Ornat eum *Phaleris*, *Frontali*, 6. *Antilena*, 7. & *Postilena*, 8.
Then he getteth upon his Horse, putteth his feet into the *Stirrops*, 9. taketh the *Bridle-rein*, 10. 11. in his left hand, wherewith he guideth and holdeth the Horse.	Deinde insilit in Equum, indit pedes *Stapedibus*, 9. capessit *Lorum* (habenam), 10. *Freni*, 11. sinistrâ quo flectit, & retinet Equum.
Then he putteth to his *Spurs*, 12. 103 and setteth him on with a *Switch*, 13. and holdeth him in with a *Musrol*, 14.	Tum admovet *Calcaria*, 12. incitatque *Virgula*, 13. & coërcet *Postomide*, 14.
The *Holsters*, 15. hang down from the *Pummel* of the *Saddle*, 16. in which the *Pistols*, 17. are put.	*Bulgæ*, 15. pendent ex *Apice Ephippii*, 16. quibus *Sclopi*, 17. inseruntur.
The Rider is clad in a short *Coat*, 18. his *Cloak* being tyed	Ipse Eques induitur *Chlamyde*, 18. *Lacernâ* revinctâ, 19.
behind him, 19. A *Post*, 20. is carried on Horseback at full Gallop.	

LXXXV.

Carriages.

Vehicula.

We are carried on *Sled*, 1. over Snow and Ice	
A Carriage with one Wheel, is called a *Wheelbarrow*, 2. 104 with two Wheels, a *Cart*, 3. with four Wheels, *Wagon*, which is either a *Timber-wagon*, or a *Load-wagon*,	
The parts of the Wagon are, the *Neep* (or draught-tree), 6. the *Beam*, 7. the *Bottom*, 8. and the *Sides*, 9. Then the *Axle-tree*, 10. about which the Wheels run, the *Lin-pins*, 11. and *Axletree-staves*, 12. being fastened before them.	
The *Nave*, 13. is the groundfast of Wheel, 14. from which come	

puero, 7. in
marmore.

The Rays of the
Sun,
burn wood
through a *Burning-
glass*, 5.

Radii Solis
accendunt ligna
per *Vitrum urens*,
5.

LXXXII.

The Roper, and the Cordwainer.

Restio, & Lorarius.

Sculptor,
& *Statuarius*
exsculpunt *Stat-
uas*, 8.
e Ligno & Lapide.
Cœlator
& *Scalptor*
insculpit *Figuras*,
10.
& *Characteres*,
Cœlo, 9.
Ligno, Æri,
liisque Metallis.

LXXXI.

The Cooper.

Vietor.

The *Roper*, 1.
100 twisteth *Cords*,
2.
of *Tow*, or *Hemp*, 4.
(which he wrappeth
about
himself)
by the turning of a
Wheel, 3.
Thus are made
first *Cords*, 5.
then *Ropes*, 6.
and at last, *Cables*,
7.

Restio, 1.
contorquet *Fu-
nes*, 2.
è *Stupa*, 4. vel
Cannabi,
quam circumdat
sibi
agitatione *Ro-
tulæ*, 3.
Sic fiunt,
primò *Funiculi*,
5.
tum *Restes*, 6.
tandem
Rudentes, 7.

Specularia, 1.
parantur, ut
homines
intueantur seip-
sos.

Perspicilla, 2.
ut cernat acius
qui habet visum
debilem.

Remota videntur
per *telescopium*,
3.
ut proxima.

Pulex, 4.
in *Microscopio*
apparet
ut porcellus.

The *Cooper*, 1.
having an *Apron*,
2.
tied about him,
maketh *Hoops*
of *Hazel-rods*, 3.
upon a *cutting-
block*, 4.
with a *Spoke-
Shave*, 5.
99 and *Lags*, 6. of
Timber,
Of *Lags* he maketh
Hogsheads, 7. and
Pipes, 8.
with two *Heads*;
and *Tubs*, 9.
Soes, 10.
Flaskets, 11.
Buckets, 12.
with one Bottom.

Then he bindeth
them
with *Hoops*, 13.
which he tyeth fast
with small *Twigs*,
15.
by means of a
Cramp-iron, 14.
and he fitteth them
on
with a *Mallet*, 16.
and a *Driver*, 17.

Vietor, 1.
amictus
Præcinctorio, 2.
facit *Circulos*,
è *Virgis Colur-
nis*, 3.
super *Sellam in-
cisoriam*, 4.
*Scalpro bi-
manubriato*, 5.
& *Assulas*, 6. ex
Ligno.
Ex Assulis con-
ficit
Dolia, 7. & *Cu-
pas*, 8.
Fundo bino;
tum *Lacus*, 9.
Labra, 10.
Pitynas [Tri-
modia], 11.
& *Situlas*, 12.
fundo uno.

Postea vincit
Circulis, 13.
quos ligat
Viminibus, 15.
ope *Falcis vi-
etoriæ*, 14.
& aptat
Tudite, 16.
ac *Tudicula*, 17.

The *Cord-wainer*,
8.
cutteth great
Thongs, 10.
Bridles, 11.
Girdles, 12.
Sword-belts, 13.
Pouches, 14.
Port-mantles, 15.
&c.
out of a *Beast-hide*,
9.

Lorarius, 8.
scindit *Lo-
ramenta*, 10.
Fræna, 11.
Cingula, 12.
Baltheos, 13.
Crumenas, 14.
Hippoperas, 15.
&c.
de *corio bubulo*,
9.

LXXXIII.

The Traveller.

Viator.

A *Traveller*, 1.

Viator, 1.

zars, 3.
or shaveth with a
Razor,
which he taketh
out of his *Case*, 4.
And he washeth one
over a *Bason*, 5.
with *Suds* running
out of a *Laver*, 6.
and also with *Sope*,
7.
and wipeth him
with a *Towel*, 8.
combeth him with a
Comb, 9.
and curleth him
with a *Crisping
Iron*, 10.
Sometimes he cut-
teth a *Vein*
with a *Pen-knife*, 11.
where the Blood
spirteth out, 12.
94 The *Chirurgeon*
cureth
Wounds.

vacuâ,
quam depromit
è *Theca*, 4.

Et lavat
super *Pelvim*,
5.
Lixivio deflu-
ente
è *Gulturnio*, 6.
ut & *Sapone*, 7.
& tergit
Linteo, 8.
pectit *Pectine*,
9.
crispat
Calamistro, 10.
Interdum secat
Venam
Scalpello, 11.
ubi *Sanguis*
propullulat, 12.
Chirurgus curat
Vulnera.

LXXVII.

The Stable.

Equile.

The *Horse-keeper*,
1.
cleaneth the *Stable*
from *Dung*, 2.

He tyeth a *Horse*, 3.
with a *Halter*, 4.
to the *Manger*, 5.
or if he apt to bite,
he maketh him fast
with a *Muzzle*, 6.

Then he streweth
Litter, 7.

Stabularius
(Equiso), 1.
purgat *Stabu-
lum*
a *Fimo*, 2.

Alligat *Equum*,
3.
Capistro, 4.
ad *Præsepe*, 5.
aut si mordax
constringit
Fiscella, 6.

Deinde suster-
nit

under him.
He *winnoweth Oats*
with a *Van*, 8.
(being mixt with
Chaff,
and taken out
of a *Chest*, 10.)
and with them
feedeth the Horse,
as also with *Hay*, 9.

95 Afterwards he
leadeth him
to the *Watering-
trough*, 11.
to water.
Then he rubbeth him
with a *Cloth*, 12.
combeth him
with a *Curry-comb*,
15.
covereth him
with an *Housing-
cloth*, 14.
and looketh upon his
Hoofs
whether the *Shoes*,
13.
be fast with the
Nails.

LXXVIII.

Dials.

Horologia.

A *Dial*
measureth Hours.

A *Sun-dial*, 1.
sheweth by the
shadow
of the *Pin*, 2.
what a *Clock* it is;
either on a Wall,
or a *Compass*, 3.

Stramenta, 7.
*Ventilat Ave-
nam*,
Vanno, 8.
(Paleis mixtam,
ac depromptam
à *Cista Pabula-
toria*, 10.)
eâque pascit
equum,
ut & *Fœno*, 9.

Postea ducit
ad *Aquarium*,
11.
aquatum.

Tum detergit
Panno, 12.
depectit
Strigili, 15.
insternit
Gausape, 14.
& inspicit
Soleas,
an *Calcei fer-
rei*, 13.
firmis *Clavis*
hæreant.

Horologium
dimetitur Ho-
ras.

Solarium, 1.
ostendit umbrâ
Gnomonis, 2.
quota sit *Hora*;
sive in Pariete,
sive in *Pyxide
Magnetica*, 3.

An *Hour-glass*, 4.
96 sheweth the fo
parts of an hour
by the running of
Sand,
heretofore of wat
A *Clock*, 5
numbereth also
the Hours of the
Night,
by the turning of
Wheels,
the greatest where
is drawn by a
Weight, 6.
and draweth the
rest.
Then either the B
7.
by its sound, bein
struck on
by the *Hammer*,
or the *Hard*, 8.
without,
by its motion abo
sheweth the hour

LXXIX.

The Picture.

Pictura.

Pictures, 1.
delight the Eyes
and adorn Rooms

The *Painter*, 2.
painteth an *Imag*
97 with a *Pencil*,
3.
in a *Table*, 4.
upon a *Case-
frame*, 5.
holding his *Pal-
let*, 6.
in his left hand,

Illuminatur
Fenestris, 4.
Calefit
Fornace, 5.
Ejus Utensilia
sunt
Scamna, 6.
Sellæ, 7.
Mensæ, 8.
cum *Fulcris*, 9.
ac *Scabellis*, 10.
& *Culcitris*, 11.
Appenduntur eti-
am
Tapetes, 12.
Pro levi cubatu,
in *Dormitorio*,
13.
est *Lectus*, (Cu-
bile) 14.
stratus in *Spon-
da*, 15.
super *Stramen-
tum*, 16.
cum *Lodicibus*,
17.
& *Stragulis*, 18.
Cervical, 19.
est sub capite.
Canopeo, 20.
Lectus tegitur.
Matula, 21.
est vesicæ
evandæ.

and they are com-
passed about
with a *Brandrith*,
2.
lest any one fall in.
Thence is water
drawn
91 with *Buckets*, 3.
hanging either at a
Pole, 4.
or a *Rope*, 5.
or a *Chain*, 6.
and that either by a
Swipe, 7.
or a *Windle*, 8.
or a *Turn*, 9.
with a *Handle*
or a *Wheel*, 10.
or to conclude,
by a *Pump*, 11.

LXXV.

The Bath.

Balneum.

& circumdantur
Crepidine, 2.
ne quis incidat.

Inde aqua haurit-
ur
Urnis (situlis), 3.
pendentibus vel
Pertica, 4.
vel *Fune*, 5.
vel *Catena*, 6.
idque aut *Tol-
lenone*, 7.
aut *Girgillo*, 8.
aut *Cylindro*, 9.
Manubriato,
aut *Rota* (tympa-
no), 10.
aut denique
Antliâ, 11.

He that desireth to
be wash'd
in cold water,
goeth down into a
River, 1.
In a *Bathing-house*,
2.
we wash off the
filth
either sitting in a
Tub, 3.
or going up
into the *Hot-house*,
4.
92 and we are
rubbed
with a *Pumice-
stone*, 6.
or a *Hair-cloth*, 5.

Qui cupit lavari
aquâ frigidâ,
descendit in *Flu-
vium*, 1.
In *Balneario*, 2.
abluimus
squalores,
sive sedentes in
Labro, 3.
sive conscen-
dentes
in *Sudatorium*,
4.
& defricamur
Pumice, 6.
aut *Cilicio*, 5.

In the *Stripping-
room*, 7.
we put off our
clothes,
and are tyed about
with an *Apron*, 8.
We cover our Head
with a *Cap*, 9.
and put our feet
into a *Bason*, 10.

The *Bath-woman*,
11.
reacheth water in a
Bucket, 12.
drawn out of the
Trough, 13.
into which it run-
neth
out of *Pipes*, 14.
The *Bath-keeper*,
15.
lanceth with a
Lancet, 16.
and by applying
Cupping-glasses,
17.
he draweth the
Blood
betwixt the skin
and the flesh,
which he wipeth
away
with a *Spunge*, 18.
93

LXXVI.

The Barbers Shop.

Tonstrina.

In *Apodyterio*, 7.
exuimus Vestes,
& præcingimur
Castula (Subli-
gari), 8.
Tegimus caput
Pileolo, 9.
& imponimus
pedes
Telluvio, 10.
Balneatrix, 11.
ministrat aquam
Situla, 12.
haustam ex
Alveo, 13.
in quem defluit
è *Canalibus*, 14.

Balneator, 15.
scarificat *Scal-
pro*, 16.
& applicando
Cucurbitas, 17.
extrahit *San-
guinem*
subcutaneum,
quem abstergit
Spongiâ, 18.

The *Barber*, 1.
in the *Barbers-shop*,
2.
cutteth off the *Hair*
and the *Beard*
with a pair of *Siz-*

Tonsor, 1.
in *Tonstrina*, 2.
tondet *Crines*
& *Barbam*
Forcipe, 3.
vel radit *No-*

Ubi *Fontes* defi-
ciunt,
Putei, 1. effodi-
untur,

Horse-shoes, 10.
Cart-strakes, 11.
Chains, 12.
Plates, Locks and Keys,
Hinges, &c.

Canthi, 11.
Catenæ, 12.
Laminæ, Seræ cum Clavibus,
Cardines. &c.

He quencheth hot Irons
in a *Cool-trough*.

Restinguit candentia,
Ferramenta in Lacu.

LXX.

The Box-maker and the Turner.

Scrinarius & Tornator.

The *Box-maker*, 1.
smootheth *hewen Boards*, 2.
with a *Plain*, 3.
upon a *work-board*, 4.
he maketh them very smooth
with a *little-plain*, 5.
he boreth them thorow
with an *Augre*, 6.
carveth them with a *Knife*, 7.
fasteneth them together
with *Glew* and *Cramp-Irons*, 8.
and maketh *Tables*, 9.
Boards, 10.
Chests, 11. &c.

The *Turner*, 12.
sitting over a *Treddle*, 13.
turneth with a *Throw*, 15.
upon a *Turner's*

Arcularius, 1.
edolat *Asseres*, 2.
Runcina, 3.
in *Tabula*, 4.
deplanat
Planula, 5.
perforat (terebrat)
Terebra, 6.
sculpit
Cultro, 7.
combinat
Glutine & *Subscudibus*, 8.
& facit *Tabulas*, 9.
Mensas, 10.
Arcus (Cistas), 11. &c.

Tornio, 12.
sedens in *Insili*, 13.
tornat *Torno*, 15.
super *Scamno*
Tornatorio, 14.

Bench, 14.
Bowls, 16. *Tops*, 17.
Puppets, 18. and such like *Turners Work*.

LXXI.

The Potter.

Figulus.

The *Potter*, 1.
sitting over a *Wheel*, 2.
maketh *Pots*, 4
Pitchers, 5.
Pipkins, 6.
Platters, 7.
Pudding-pans, 8.
Juggs, 9.
Lids, 10. &c.
of *Potter's Clay*, 3.
afterwards he baketh them in an *Oven*, 11.
and glazeth them with *White Lead*.

A broken Pot affordeth *Pot-sheards*, 1

Figulus, 1.
sedens super *Rota*, 2.
format *Ollas*, 4.
Urceos, 5.
Tripodes, 6.
Patinas, 7.
Vasa testacea, 8.
Fidelias, 9.
Opercula, 10. &c.
ex *Argillâ*, 3.
postea excoquit in *Furno*, 11.
& incrustat *Lithargyro*.

Fracta Olla dat *Testas*, 12.

LXXII.

The Parts of a House.

Partes Domus.

Globos, 16.
Conos, 17.
Icunculas, 18. & similia *Toreumata*.

A *House* is divided into inner *Rooms*,
such as are the *Entry*, 1.
the *Stove*, 2.
the *Kitchen*, 3.
the *Buttery*, 4.
the *Dining Room*, 5.
the *Gallery*, 6.
the *Bed Chamber*, 7.
with a *Privy*, 8. made by it.
Baskets, 9. are of use for carrying things,
and *Chests*, 10. (which are made fast with a *Key*, 11.) for keeping them.

Under the *Roof*, is the *Floor*, 12.

In the *Yard*, 13. is a *Well*, 14.
a *Stable*, 15. and a *Barn*, 16.

Under the House is the *Cellar*, 17.

LXXIII.

The Stove with the Hypocaustum cu

The *Stove*, 1. is beautified with an *Arched Roof*, 2.
and wainscoted

estibulum, 1.
t ante *Januam*
omûs.

nua habet
men, 2.
Superliminare,
3.
Postes, 4.
rinque.
ardines, 5.
nt a dextris,
quibus pendent
ores, 6.
austrum, 7.
t Pessulus, 8.
sinistris.

b ædibus
t Cavædium, 9.
vimento
ssellato, 10.
citum Columnis,

quibus Peristyli-
, 12.
Basis, 13.

scenditur in su-
riores
ntignationes per
alas, 14.
Cochlidia, 15.

nestræ, 16.
parent extrinse-
s,

outside,
and the *Grates*,
17.
the *Galleries*, 18.
the *Watertables*,
19.
the *Butteresses*,
20.
to bear up the
walls.

On the top is the
Roof, 21.
covered with
Tyles, 22.
or *Shingles*, 23.
which lie upon
Laths, 24.
and these upon
Rafters, 25.

The *Eaves*, 26.
adhere to the
Roof.

The place with-
out a Roof
is called an *open
Gallery*, 27.

In the Roof are
Jettings out, 28.
and *Pinnacles*,
29.

84

& *Cancelli*
(clathra), 17.
Pergulæ, 18.
Suggrundia, 19.
& *Fulcra*, 20.
fulciendis muris.

In summo est *Tec-
tum*, 21.
contectum *Imbri-
cibus* (tegulis), 22.
vel *Scandulis*, 23.
quæ incumbunt
Tigillis, 24.
hæc *Tignis*, 25.

Tecto adhæret
Stillicidium, 26.

Locus sine Tecto
dicitur *Subdiale*,
27.

In Tecto sunt
Meniana, 28.
& *Coronides*, 29.

LXVIII.

A Mine.

Metallifodina.

Miners, 1.
go into the *Grave*,
2.
by a *Stick*, 3. or
by *Ladders*, 4.
with *Lanthorns*,
5.
and dig out with a
Pick, 6.

Metalli fossores,
1.
ingrediuntur *Pu-
teum fodinæ*, 2.
Bacillo, 3. sive
Gradibus, 4.
cum *Lucernis*, 5.
& effodiunt
Ligone, 6.

the *Oar*,
which being put
in *Baskets*, 7.
is drawn out with
a *Rope*, 8.
by means of a
Turn, 9.
and is carried
to the *Melting-
house*, 10.
where it is forced
with fire,
that the *Metal*
may run out, 12.
the *Dross*, 11.
is thrown aside.

85

terram *Metalli-
cam*,
quæ imposita
Corbibus, 7.
extrahitur *Fune*,
8.
ope *Machinæ
tractoriæ*, 9.
& defertur
in *Ustrinam*, 10.
ubi urgetur igne,
ut *Metallum*, 12.
profluat
Scoriæ, 11. abjici-
untur
seorsim.

LXIX.

The Blacksmith.

Faber Ferrarius.

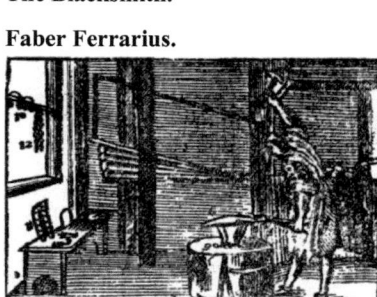

The *Blacksmith*,
1.
in his *Smithy* (or
Forge), 2.
bloweth the fire
with a *pair of
Bellows*, 3.
which he bloweth
with his *Feet*, 4.
and so heateth the
Iron:

And then he
taketh it out
with the *Tongs*, 5.
layeth it upon the
Anvile, 6.
and striketh it
with an *Hammer*,
7.
where the *sparks*,
8. fly off.

And thus are
hammer'd out,
Nails, 9.

Faber ferrarius, 1.
in *Ustrina* (Fab-
ricâ), 2.
inflat ignem
Folle, 3.
quem adtollit
Pede, 4.
atq; ita candefacit
Ferrum:

Deinde eximit
Forcipe, 5.
imponit *Incudi*, 6.
& cudit
Malleo, 7.
ubi *Stricturæ*, 8.
exiliunt.

Et sic excuduntur,
Clavi, 9.
Solea, 10.

Man's food and clothing: now his Dwelling followeth.
At first they dwelt in *Caves*, 1. then in *Booths* or *Huts*, 2. and then again in *Tents*, 3. at the last in *Houses*.

The *Woodman* felleth and heweth down *Trees*, 5. with an *Ax*, 4. the *Boughs*, 6. remaining.

He cleaveth *Knotty Wood* with a *Wedge*, 7. which he forceth in with a *Beetle*, 8. and maketh *Wood-stacks*, 9.

The *Carpenter* squareth *Timber* with a *Chip-Ax*, 10.

80 whence *Chips*, 11. fall, and saweth it with a *Saw*, 12. where the *Saw-dust*, 13. falleth down.

Afterwards he lifteth the *Beam* upon *Tressels*, 14. by the help of a *Pully*, 15. fasteneth it with *Cramp-irons*, 16. and marketh it out with a *Line*, 17

Thus he frameth the *Walls* togeth-

& amictum, vidimus sequitur nunc Domicilium ejus.
Primò habitabant in *Speluous*, 1. deinde in *Tabernaculis* vel *Tuguriis*, 2. tum etiam in *Tentoriis*, 3. demum in *Domibus*.

Lignator sternit & truncat *Arbores*, 5. *Securi*, 4. remanentibus *Sarmentis*, 6.

Findit *Nodosum*, *Lignum Cuneo*, 7. quem adigit *Tudite*, 8. & componit *Strues*, 9.

Faber Lignarius ascit *Ascia*, 10. *Materiam*, unde *Assulæ*, 11. cadunt, & serrat *Serrâ*, 12. ubi *Scobs*, 13. decidit.

Post elevat *Tignum* super *Canterios*, 14. ope *Trochleæ*, 15. affigit *Ansis*, 16. & lineat *Amussi*, 17.

Tum compaginat *Parietes*, 18.

er, 18. and fasteneth the great pieces with *Pins*, 19.

LXV.
The Mason.
Faber Murarius.

The *Mason*, 1. layeth a *Foundation*, and buildeth *Walls*, 2. Either of *Stones* which the *Stone-digger* getteth out of the *Quarry*, 3. 81 and the *Stone-cutter*, 4. squareth by a *Rule*, 5.

Or of *Bricks*, 6. which are made of *Sand* and *Clay* steeped in water, and are burned in fire.

Afterwards he plaistereth it with *Lime*, by means of a *Trowel*, and garnisheth with a *Rough-cast*, 8.

LXVI.
Engines.
Machinæ.

One can carry as much by thrust-

& configit trabes *Clavis trabalibus*, 19.

Faber Murarius, 1. ponit *Fundamentum*, & struit *Muros*, 2. Sive è *Lapidibus*, quos *Lapidarius* eruit in *Lapicidina*, 3. & *Latomus*, 4. conquadrat ad *Normam*, 5.

Sive è *Lateribus*, 6. qui formantur, ex *Arena* & *Luto*, aquâ intritis & excoquuntur igne.

Dein crustat *Calce*, ope *Trullæ*, 7. & vestit *Tectorio*, 8.

Unus potest ferre tantum trudendo

ing a *Wheel-borrow*, before him, (having an *Harness*, 4. hanging on his neck,) as two men can carry on a *Colestaff*, 1. or *Hand-barrow*, 2.

82 But he can do more that rolleth a *Weight* laid upon *Rollers*, 6. with a *Leaver*, 5.

A *Wind-beam*, 7. is a post, which is turned by going about it.

A *Crane*, 8. hath a *Hollow-wheel*, in which one walking draweth weights out of a *Ship*, or letteth them down into a *Ship*.

A *Rammer*, 9. is used to fasten *Piles*, 10. it is lifted with a *Rope* drawn by *Pullies* 11. or with hands, if it have *handles* 12.

4. pedibus.
Diducit *Stamen*, 5.
Liciis,
& trajicit *Radium*, 6.
in quo est *Trama*,
ac densat.
Pectine, 7.
atque ita conficit *Linteum*, 8.
Sic etiam *Pannifex*
facit *Pannum* è *Lana*.

Linteamina insolantur, 1.
aquâ perfusâ, 2.
donec candefiant.

Ex iis *Sartrix*, 3.
suit *Indusia*, 4.
Muccinia, 5.
Collaria, 6.
Capitia, &c.
Haec, si sordidentur lavantur rursum,
a *Lotrice*, 7.
aquâ,
sive *Lixivio* ac *Sapone*.

LXII.

The Taylor.
Sartor.

The *Taylor*, 1. cutteth
Cloth, 2. with
Shears, 3.
and seweth it together with a *Needle*
and *double thread*,
Then he presseth the *Seams*
with a *Pressing-iron*, 5.
And thus he maketh *Coats*, 6.
with *Plaits*, 7.
in which the *Border*, 8. is below
with *Laces*, 9.
Cloaks, 10.
with a *Cape*, 11.
and *Sleeve Coats*, 12.

Doublets, 13.
with *Buttons*, 14.
and *Cuffs*, 15.

Breeches, 16.
sometimes with *Ribbons*, 17.
Stockins, 18.
Gloves, 19.
78 *Muntero Caps*, 20. &c.
So the *Furrier*
maketh *Furred Garments*
of *Furs*.

Sartor, 1. discindit
Pannum, 2.
Forfice, 3.
consuitque *Acu* & *Filo duplicato*, 4.

Posteâ complanat *Suturas*
Ferramento, 5.

Sicque conficit *Tunicas*, 6.
Plicatas, 7.
in quibus infra est *Fimbria*, 8.
cum *Institis*, 9.
Pallia, 10.
cum *Patagio*, 11.
& *Togas Manicatas*, 12.

Thoraces, 13.
cum *Globulis*, 14.
& *Manicis*, 15.

Caligas, 16.
aliquando cum *Lemniscis*, 17.
Tibialia, 18.
Chirothecas, 19.
Amiculum, 20. &c.

Sic *Pellio*
facit *Pellicia*
è *Pellibus*.

LXIII.

The Shoemaker.
Sutor.

The *Shoemaker*, 1.
maketh *Slippers*, 7.
Shoes, 8.
(in which is seen
above, the *Upper-leather*,
beneath the *Sole*,
and on both sides
the *Latchets*)
Boots, 9.
and *High Shoes*, 10.
of *Leather*, 5.
(which is cut with
a *Cutting-knife*), 6.
by means of an *Awl*, 2.
and *Lingel*, 3.
upon a *Last*, 4.
79

Sutor, 1.
conficit *Crepidas* (Sandalia,) 7.
Calceos, 8.
(in quibus spectatur superne *Obstragulum*,
inferne *Solea*,
et utrinque *Ansæ*)
Ocreas, 9.
et *Perones*, 10.
e *Corio*, 5.
(quod discinditur *Scalpro Sutorio*, 6.)
ope *Subulæ*, 2.
et Fili *picati*, 3.
super *Modum*, 4.

LXIV.

The Carpenter.
Faber lignarius.

We have seen   Hominis victum

become *Vinegar*.
Of Wine and Honey
they make *Mead*.

fiunt *Acetum*.
Ex Vino &
Melle
faciunt *Mulsum*.

LVIII.

A Feast.

Convivium.

When a *Feast*
is made ready,
the table is covered
with a *Carpet*, 1.
73 and a *Table-
cloth*, 2.
by the *Waiters*,
who besides lay
the *Trenchers*, 3.
Spoons, 4.
Knives, 5.
with little *Forks*, 6.
Table-napkins, 7
Bread, 8.
with a *Salt-seller*,
9.

Cum *Convivium*
apparatur,
Mensa sternitur
Tapetibus, 1.
& *Mappa*, 2.
à *Triciniariis*,
qui præterea opponunt
Discos (Orbes),
3.
Cochlearia, 4.
Cultros, 5.
cum *Fuscinulis*,
6.
Mappulas, 7.
Panem, 8.
cum *Salino*, 9.

Messes are brought
in *Platters*, 10.
a *Pie*, 19. on a
Plate.

Fercula inferuntur
in *Patinis*, 10.
Artocrea, 19. in
Lance.

The Guests being
brought in
by the *Host*, 11.
wash their Hands
out of a *Laver*, 12.
or *Ewer*, 14.
over a *Hand-basin*,
13.
or *Bowl*, 15.
and wipe them
on a *Hand-towel*,
16.
then they sit at the
Table
on *Chairs*, 17.

Convivæ introducti
ab *Hospite*, 11.
abluunt manus
è *Gutturnio*, 12.
vel *Aquali*, 14.
super *Malluvium*, 13.
aut *Pelvim*, 15.
terguntque
Mantili, 16.
tum assident
Mensæ
per *Sedilia*, 17.

The *Carver*, 18.
breaketh up the
good Cheer,
and divideth it.
Sauces are set
amongst
Roast-meat, in
Sawcers, 20.
The *Butler*, 21.
filleth *strong Wine*
out of a *Cruise*, 25.
or *Wine-pot*, 26.
or *Flagon*, 27.
into *Cups*, 22.
or *Glasses*, 23.
which stand
on a *Cupboard*, 24.
and he reacheth
them
to the *Master of
the Feast*, 28.
who drinketh to his
Guests.
74

Structor, 18.
deartuat dapes,
& distribuit.
Embammata interponuntur
Assutaris in
Scutellis, 20.
Pincerna, 21.
infundit *Temetum*,
ex *Urceo*, 25.
vel *Canthara*,
26.
vel *Lagena*, 27.
in *Pocula*, 22.
vel *Vitrea*, 23.
quæ extant
in *abaco*, 24.
& porrigit,
Convivatori, 28.
qui propinat
Hospitibus.

LIX.

The Dressing of Line.

Tractatio Lini.

Line and *Hemp*
being rated in
water,
and dryed again,
1.
are braked
with a *wooden
Brake*, 2.
where the *Shives*, 3.
fall down,
then they are
heckled
with an *Iron
Heckle*, 4.
where the *Tow*,

Linum & Cannabis,
macerata aquis,
et siccata rursum,
1.
contunduntur
Frangibulo ligneo,
2.
ubi *Cortices*, 3.
decidunt
tum carminantur
Carmine ferreo, 4.
ubi *Stupa*, 5.
separatur.

5.
is parted from it.
Flax is tyed to a
Distaff, 6.
by the *Spinster*,
7.
which with her
left hand
pulleth out the
Thread, 8.
and with her
right hand
turneth a *Wheel*,
9.
or a *Spindle*, 10.
upon which is a
Wharl, 11.
The *Spool* receiveth
the *Thread*, 13.
75 which is
drawn thence
upon a *Yarn-
windle*, 14
hence either
Clews, 15.
are wound up,
or *Hanks*, 16.
are made.

LX.

Weaving.

Textura.

The *Webster*
undoeth the *Clew*
into *Warp*,
and wrappeth it at
the *Beam*, 2
and as he sitteth
in his *Loom*, 3.
he treadeth upon
Treddles, 4.
with his Feet.

dem carnes
Lardo, ope
Creacentri, 7.

Lepores, 8. exuit,
tum elixat *Ollis*,
9.
& *Cacabis*, 10.
in *Foco*, 11.
& despumat
Lingula, 12.

Condit
elixata, Aromatibus,
quæ comminuit
Pistillo, 14. in
Mortario, 13.
aut terit *Radulâ*,
15.

Quædam assat
Verubus, 16.
& *Automato*, 17.
vel super *Craticulum*, 18.

Vel frigit
Sartagine, 19.
super *Tripodem*,
20.

Vasa Coquinaria
præterea sunt,
Rutabulum, 21.
Foculus (Ignitabulum), 22.
Trua, 23.
(in quâ *Catini*,
24. &
Patinæ, 25. eluuntur)
Forceps, 26.
Culter incisorius, 27.
Qualus, 28.
Corbis, 29.
& *Scopa*, 30.

LVI.
The Vintage.
Vindemia.

Wine groweth
in the *Vine-yard*, 1.
where *Vines* are
propagated
and tyed with
Twigs
to *Trees*, 2.
or to *Props*, 3.
or *Frames*, 4.

When the time of
Grape-gathering is
come,
they cut off the
Bunches,
and carry them in
*Measures of three
Bushels*, 5.
and throw them into
a *Vat*, 6.
and tread them
with their *Feet*, 7.
or stamp them
with a *Wooden-
Pestil*, 8.
and squeeze out the
juice
in a *Wine-press*, 9.
which is called
Must, 11.
71 and being received
in a great *Tub*, 10.
it is poured into
Hogsheads, 12.
it is stopped up, 15.
and being laid close
in *Cellars*
upon *Settles*, 14.
it becometh *Wine*.
It is drawn out of

Vinum crescit
in *Vinea*, 1.
ubi *Vites* propagantur,
& alligantur viminibus
ad *Arbores*, 2.
vel ad *Palos*
(ridicas), 3.
vel ad *Juga*, 4

Cùm tempus
vindemiandi
adest,
abscindunt
Botros,
& comportant
Trimodiis, 5.
conjiciuntque in
Lacum, 6.
calcant
Pedibus, 7.
aut tundunt
Ligneo Pilo, 8.
& exprimunt
succum
Torculari, 9.
qui dicitur *Mustum*, 11.
& exceptum
Orcâ, 10.
infunditur
Vasis (Doliis),
12.
operculatur, 15.
& abditum in
Cellis,
super *Cantherios*, 14.
abit in *Vinum*.

Promitur e *Do-*

the *Hogshead*,
with a *Cock*, 13.
or *Faucet*, 16.
(in which is a *Spigot*)
the Vessel being
unbunged.

LVII.
Brewing.
Zythopœia.

Where *Wine* is not
to be had
they drink *Beer*,
which is brewed of
Malt, 1.
and *Hops*, 2.
in a *Caldron*, 3.
afterwards it is
poured
into *Vats*, 4.
72 and when it is
cold,
it is carried in *Soes*,
5.
into the *Cellar*, 6.
and is put into Vessels.

Brandy-wine,
extracted by the
power of heat
from dregs of Wine
in a *Pan*, 7.
over which a *Limbeck*, 8.
is placed,
droppeth through a
Pipe, 9.
into a *Glass*.

Wine and Beer
when they turn
sowre,

lio
Siphone, 13.
aut *Tubulo*, 16.
(in quo est *Epistomium*)
Vase relito.

Ubi *Vinum* non
habetur,
bibitur *Cerevisia*
(*Zythus*),
quæ coquitur ex
Byne, 1.
& *Lupulo*, 2.
in *Aheno*, 3.
post effunditur
in *Lacus*, 4.
& frigefactum,
defertur *Labris*,
5.
in *Cellaria*, 6.
& intunditur vasibus.

Vinum sublimatum,
extractum vi
Caloris
e fecibus Vini
in *Aheno*, 7.
cui *Alembicum*,
8.
superimpositum
est,
destillat per
Tubum, 9.
in *Vitrum*.

Vinum & Cerevisia,
cum acescunt,

over,
in his net whilst
they settle themselves down.

Or he setteth
Snares, 8.
on which they
hang and
strangle themselves:

Or setteth Limetwigs, 9.
on a Perch, 10.
66 upon which if
they sit
they enwrap their
Feathers,
so that they cannot fly away,
and fall down to
the ground.

Or he catcheth
them
with a Pole, 11.
or a Pit-fall, 12.

Aut tendit Tendiculas, 8.
quibus suspendunt
&
suffocant seipsas:

Aut exponit Viscatos calamos, 9.
Amiti, 10.
quibus si insident,
implicant pennas,
ut nequeant
avolare,
& decidunt in terram.

Aut captat
Perticâ, 11.
vel Decipulâ, 12.

LIII.

Hunting.

Venatus.

The Hunter, 1.
hunteth wild Beasts
whilst he besetteth a
Wood
with Toyls, 2.
stretched out upon
Shoars, 3.

The Beagle, 4.
tracketh the wild
Beast
or findeth him out by
the scent;
the Tumbler, or Greyhound, 5.

Venator, 1.
venatur Feras,
dum cingit
Sylvam,
Cassibus, 2.
tentis super
Varos, 3. (furcillas.)

Canis sagax,
4.
vestigat Feram,
aut indagat
odoratu;
Vertagus, 5.

pursueth it.
The Wolf,
falleth in a Pit, 6.
67 the Stag, 7. as he
runneth away,
into Toyls.

The Boar, 8.
is struck through
with a Hunting-spear, 9.
The Bear, 10.
is bitten by Dogs,
and is knocked
with a Club, 11.

If any thing get
away,
it escapeth, 12 as
here
a Hare and a Fox.

LIV.

Butchery.

Lanionia.

The Butcher, 1.
killeth fat Cattle,
2.
(The Lean, 3.
are not fit to eat.)

He knocketh them
down
with an Ax, 4
or cutteth their
Throat,
68 with a Slaughter-knife, 5.
he flayeth them, 6.
and cutteth them
in pieces,
and hangeth out
the flesh
to sell in the

persequitur.
Lupus,
incidit in
Foveam, 6.
fugiens
Cervus, 7.
in Plagas.

Aper, 8.
transverberatur
Venabulo, 9.

Ursus, 10.
mordetur à
Canibus,
& tunditur
Clavâ, 11.

Si quid effugit,
evadit, 12. ut
hic
Lepus &
Vulpes.

Lanio, 1.
mactat Pecudem
altilem, 2.
(Vescula, 3.
non sunt vescenda.)

Prosternit
Clavâ, 4.
vel jugulat.
Cunaculo, 5.
excoriat (deglubit,) 6.
dissecatque
& exponit carnes,
venum in Macello, 7.

Shambles, 7.
He dresseth a
Swine, 8.
with fire
or scalding water
9.
and maketh Gamons, 10.
Pistils, 11.
and Flitches, 12.
Besides several
Puddings,
Chitterlings, 13.
Bloodings 14.
Liverings, 15.
Sausages, 16.

The Fat, 17. and
Tallow, 18. are
melted.

LV.

Cookery.

Coquinaria.

The Yeoman of the
Larder, 1.
bringeth forth Provision, 2.
out of the Larder
3.
69 The Cook, 4.
taketh them
and maketh several
Meats.

He first pulleth off
the Feathers
and draweth the
Gutts
out of the Birds,
He scaleth and
splitteth Fish, 6.

He draweth some

Mola,	in a *Rindge*, 2.	*Cribo*, 2. (pollinario)
...pis, 2. currit	and putteth it into	
per lapidem, 3.	the *Kneading-trough*, 3.	& indit *Mactræ*, 3.
...ta, 4.	Then he poureth water to it	Tum affundit aquam,
...cumagente, et	and maketh	& facit *Massam*, 4.
...nterit grana in-	*Dough*, 4.	
...sa	and kneadeth it	depsitque
...*Infundibulum*,	with a *wooden slice*, 5.	*spatha*, 5. ligneâ.
...aratque *Fur-*	Then he maketh	Dein format
...em, 6.	*Loaves*, 6. *Cakes*, 7.	*Panes*, 6. *Placentas*, 7.
...cidentem in *Cis-*	*Cimnels*, 8. *Rolls*, 9. &c.	*Similas*, 8. *Spiras*, 9. &c.
...n, 7.	Afterwards he setteth them	Post imponit
...*arina* (Polline)	on a *Peel*, 10.	*Palæ*, 10.
...bente per *Excus-*	and putteth them	& ingerit
...*rium*, 8.	thorow the *Oven-mouth*, 12.	*Furno*, 11. per *Præfurnium*, 12.
...is Mola primùm	into the *Oven*, 11.	
...*inuaria*, 9.	But first he pulleth out	Sed priùs eruit ignem & Carbones
...inde *Jumentaria*,	the fire and the Coals	*Rutabulo*, 13.
	with a *Coal-rake*, 13.	quos congerit infra, 14.
...*Aquatica*, 11.	64 which he layeth	
...*Navalis*, 12.	on a heap	
...dem, *Alata*	underneath, 14.	
...eumatica), 13.	And thus is *Bread* baked,	Et sic *Panis* pinsitur
	having the *Crust* without, 15.	habens extra *Crustam*, 15.
	and the *Crumb* within, 16.	intus *Micam*, 16.

LI.

Fishing.

Piscatio.

...istor, 1.	The *Fisher-man*, 1.	*Piscator*, 1.
...ernit *Farinam*	catcheth fish,	captat pisces,

either on the Shoar, with an *Hook*, 2. which hangeth by a *Line* from the *angling-rod*, on which the *Bait* sticketh; or with a *Cleek-net*, 3. which hangeth on a *Pole*, 4. is put into the Water; or in a *Boat*, 5. with a *Trammel-net*, 6. or with a *Wheel*, 7. which is laid in the Water by Night.

sive in littore, *Hamo*, 2. qui pendet *filo* ab *arundine*, & cui *Esca* inhæret; sive *Fundâ*, 3. quæ pendens *Pertica*, 4. immittitur aquæ; sive in *Cymba*, 5. *Reti*, 6. sive *Nassa*, 7. quæ demergitur per Noctem.

LII.

Fowling.

Aucupium.

The *Fowler*, 1. maketh a *Bed*, 2. spreadeth a *Bird-net*, 3. throweth a *Bait*, 4. upon it, and hiding himself in a *Hut*, 5. he allureth Birds, by the chirping of *Lurebirds*, which partly hop upon the Bed, 6. and are partly shut in *Cages*, 7. and thus he entangleth Birds that fly

Auceps, 1. exstruit *Aream*, 2. superstruit illi *Rete* aucupatorium, 3. obsipat *Escam*, 4. & abdens se in *Latibulo*, 5. allicit Aves, cantu *Illicum*, qui partim in Area currunt, 6. partim inclusi sunt *Caveis*, 7. atque ita obruit transvolantes Aves *Reti*, dum se demittunt:

afore
with *Dung*, 8.)
with a *Share*, 7.
and a *Coulter*,
and maketh *furrows*,
9.

Then he *soweth*
the *Seed*, 10.
and harroweth it in
with a *Harrow*, 11.
The *Reaper*, 12.
sheareth the ripe
corn
with a *Sickle*, 13.
gathereth up the
handfuls, 14.
59 and bindeth the
Sheaves, 15.

The *Thrasher*, 16.
thrasheth Corn
on the *Barn-floor*,
17.
with a *Flayl*, 18. tosseth
it in a *winnowing-basket*, 19.
and so when the
Chaff,
and the *Straw*, 20.
are separated from
it,
he putteth it into
Sacks, 12.

The *Mower*, 22.
maketh *Hay* in a
Meadow,
cutting down *Grass*
with a *Sithe*, 23.
and raketh it together
with a *Rake*, 24. and
maketh up *Cocks*,
26.
with a *fork*, 25. and
carrieth it on *Carriages*, 27.
into the *Hay-barn*,
28.

XLVII.

Grasing.

Pecuaria.

60 *Tillage of*

Vomere, 7.
et *Dentali*,
facitque *Sulcos*,
9.

Tum *seminat*
Semen, 10.
& inoccat
Occâ, 11.
Messor, 12.
metit fruges
maturas
Falce messoris,
13.
colligit *Manipulos*, 14.
& colligat *Mergetes*, 15.

Tritor, 16.
triturat frumentum
in *Area Horrei*,
17.
Flagello (tribula), 18.
jactat *ventilabro*, 19.
atque ita *Paleâ*
& *Stramine*, 20.
separatâ,
congerit in *Saccos*, 21.

Fœniseca, 22.
facit *Fœnum* in
Prato,
desecans *Gramen*,
Falce fœnaria,
23.
corraditque
Rastro, 24.
componit *Acervos*, 26.
Furca, 25. &
convehit *Vehibus*, 27.
in *Fœnile*, 28.

Cultus Agro-

ground,
and keeping *Cattle*,
was in old time
the care of *Kings*
and *Noble-men*,
at this Day only
of the meanest sort
of People,

The *Neat-heard*, 1.
calleth out the
Heards, 2.
out of the *Beast-houses*, 3.
with a *Horn*, 4.
and driveth them to
feed.
The *Shepherd*, 5.
feedeth his *Flock*, 6.
being furnished with
a
Pipe, 7. and a *Scrip*,
8.
and a *Sheep-hook*,
9.
having with him
a great *Dog*, 10.
fenced with a *Collar*, 11.
against the *Wolves*.
Swine, 12. are fed
out of a *Swine-Trough*.

The *Farmer's Wife*,
13.
milketh the *Udders*
of the *Cow*, 15.
at the *Cratch*, 15.
over a *milk-pale*, 16.
and maketh *Butter*
of *Cream*
in a *Churn*, 17.
and *Cheeses*, 18.
of *Curds*.

rum,
& *res pecuaria*,
antiquissimis
temporibus,
erat cura
Regum, Heroum;
hodie tantum
infirmæ Plebis,

Bubulcus, 1.
evocat *Armenta*, 2.
è *Bovilibus*, 3.
Buccina (Cornu), 4,
& ducit pastum.

Opilio (Pastor),
5.
pascit *Gregem*,
6.
instructus *Fistula*, 7.
& *Pera*, 8.
ut & *Pedo*, 9.
habens secum
Molossum, 10.
munitum *Millo*,
11.
contra Lupos.
Sues, 12. saginantur
ex *aqualiculo*
haræ.

Villica, 13.
mulget *Ubera*
vaccæ, 14.
ad *Præsepe*, 15.
super *mulctra*,
16.
et facit *Butyrum*
è *flore lactis*,
in *Vase butyraceo*, 17.
et *Caseos*, 18.
è *Coagulo*.

The *Wool*, 19.
is shorn from *Sheep*
whereof several
Garments
are made.

XLVIII.

The making of Honey

Mellificium.

The *Bees* send out
a *swarm*, 1. and set
over it
a *Leader*, 2.

That swarm
being ready to fly
away
is recalled by the
Tinkling
of a *brazen Vessel*,
3.
and is put up
into a new *Hive*, 4.
They make little
Cells
with six corners, 5
and fill them with
Honey-dew,
and make *Combs*,
6.
out of which the
Honey
runneth, 7.
The *Partitions*
being melted by
fire,
turn into *Wax*, 8.

XLIX.

Grinding.

Molitura.

lor,
in passione.
Vera cognitio
rei, est *Scientia*;
falsa, *Error*,
Opinio, *Suspicio*.

strous People.

osi.

*Monstrosi, &
deformes* sunt
abeuntes corpore
à communi formâ,
ut sunt, immanis
Gigas,
nanus
(*Pumilio*), 2.
Bicorpor, 3.
Biceps, 4.
& id genus
monstra.

His accensentur,
Capito, 5.
Naso, 6.
Labeo, 7.
Bucco, 8.
Strabo, 9.
Obstipus, 10.
Strumosus, 11.
Gibbosus, 12.
Loripes, 13.
Cilo, 15.
adde
Calvastrum, 14.

13.
The *steeple-crowned*, 15.
add to these
The *Bald-pated*, 14.

XLV.

The Dressing of Gardens.

Hortorum cultura.

We have seen
Man:
Now let us go on to
57 Man's *living,*
and to
Handy-craft-Trades,
which tend to it.
The first and most ancient
sustenance, were
the
Fruits of the Earth.
Hereupon the first labour of Adam,
was
the dressing of a garden.
The *Gardener*, 1.
diggeth in a *Garden-plot*,
with a *Spade*, 2.
or *Mattock*, 3.
and maketh *Beds*, 4.
and places wherein to plant *Trees*, 5.
on which he setteth
Seeds and *Plants*.
The *Tree-Gardener*, 6.
planteth Trees, 7.
in an *Orchard*,

Vidimus
hominem:
Jam pergamus ad
Victum hominis,
& ad
Artes Mechanicas,
quæ huc faciunt.
Primus & antiquissimus
Victus, erant
Fruges Terræ.
Hinc primus
Labor Adami,
Horti cultura.

Hortulanus (Olitor), 1.
fodit in *Viridario,*
Ligone, 2.
aut *Bipalio*, 3.
facitque *Pulvinos*, 4.
ac *Plantaria*, 5.
quibus inserit
Semina & *Plantas.*

Arborator, 6.
plantat Arbores, 7.
in *Pomario,*

and grafteth
Cyons, 8.
in *Stocks*, 9.
He fenceth his Garden,
either by care,
with a *mound*, 10.
or a *Stone-wall*, 11.
or a *rail*, 12.
or *Pales*, 13.
or a *Hedge*, 14.
made of *Hedge-stakes,*
and *bindings;*
Or by Nature, with
Brambles and *Bryers*, 15.
It is beautified
with *Walks*, 16.
and *Galleries*, 17.
It is watered
with *Fountains*, 18.
and a *Watering-pot*, 19.
58

XLVI.

Husbandry.

Agricultura.

The *Plow-man*, 1.
yoketh *Oxen*, 3.
to a *Plough*, 2.
and holding the
Plow-stilt, 4.
in his left hand,
and the *Plow-staff*, 5.
in his right hand,
with which he removeth
Clods, 6.
he cutteth the Land,
(which was manured

inseritque *Surculos*, 8.
Viviradicibus, 9.
Sepit hortum
vel Cura,
Muro, 10.
aut *Macerie*, 11.
aut *Vacerra*, 12.
aut *Plancis*, 13.
aut *Sepe*, 14.
flexâ è *sudibus*
& *vitilibus;*

Vel Natura
Dumis &
Vepribus, 15.
Ornatur
Ambulacris, 16.
& *Pergulis*, 17.
Rigatur
Fontanis, 18.
& *Harpagio*, 19.

Arator, 1.
jungit *Boves*, 3.
Aratro, 2.
& tenens *Stivam*, 4.
lævâ,
Rallum, 5.
dextrâ,
quâ amovet
Glebas, 6.
scindit terram
(stercoratam
antea
Fimo, 8.)

the *lesser Bone* in the Arm.
52 The *Thigh-bone*, 14.
the foremost, 16.
and the hindmost Bone,
in the Leg, 17.
The Bones of the Hand, 18.
are thirty-four, and of the Foot, 19. thirty.
The *Marrow* is in the Bones.

Tibia, 14.
Fibula, 16. anterior,
& posterior, 17.
Ossa Manûs, 18. sunt triginta quatuor,
Pedis, 19. triginta.
Medulla est in Ossibus.

XLII.

The Outward and Inward Senses.

Sensus externi & interni.

There are five outward *Senses*;
The *Eye*, 1. seeth Colours,
what is white or black,
green or blew,
red or yellow.

Sunt quinque externi *Sensus*;
Oculus, 1. videt Colores,
quid album vel atrum,
viride vel cœruleum,
rubrum aut luteum, sit.

The *Ear*, 2. heareth Sounds, both natural,
Voices and Words; and artificial,
53 Musical Tunes.
The *Nose*, 3. scenteth
smells and stinks.
The *Tongue*, 4. with the roof of the Mouth
tastes *Savours*,
what is sweet or

Auris, 2. audit Sonos, tum naturales
Voces & Verba; tum artificiales,
Tonos Musicos.
Nasus, 3. olfacit odores & fœtores.
Lingua, 4. cum Palato gustat Sapores,
quid dulce aut amarum,

bitter,
keen or biting,
sower or harsh.
The *Hand*, 5. by touching
discerneth the quantity
and quality of things;
the hot and cold,
the moist and dry,
the hard and soft,
the smooth and rough,
the heavy and light.
The inward *Senses* are three.
The *Common Sense*, 7.
under the *forepart of the head*, apprehendeth
things taken from the outward Senses.
The *Phantasie*, 6. under the *crown of the head*
judgeth of those things,
thinketh and dreameth.
The *Memory*, 8. under the *hinder part of the head*, layeth up every thing
and fetcheth them out:
it loseth some,
and this is *forgetfulness*.
Sleep, is
the rest of the Senses.
54

XLIII.

The Soul of Man.

Anima hominis.

acre aut acidum,
acerbum aut austerum.
Manus, 5. tangendo
dignoscit quantitatem,
& qualitatem rerum;
calidum & frigidum,
humidum & siccum,
durum & molle,
læve & asperum,
grave & leve.
Sensus interni sunt tres.

Sensus Communis, 7.
sub sincipite apprehendit res perceptas a Sensibus externis.

Phantasia, 6.
sub vertice,
dijudicat res istas,
cogitat, somniat.

Memoria, 8.
sub occipitio,
recondit singula & depromit:
deperdit quædam,
& hoc est oblivio.

Somnus, est requies Sensuum.

The *Soul* is the L... of the Body, one the whole.
Only *Vegetative* i *Plants*;

Withal *Sensitive* Animals;

And also rational Men.

This consisteth in three things;
In the *Understanding*,
whereby it judge[s] and understandet[h]
a thing good and evil,
or true, or appare[nt]

In the *Will*,
whereby it chooseth
and desireth,
or rejecteth, and misliketh a thing known.
In the *Mind*,
whereby it pursu...
55 the Good cho[seth]
or
avoideth the Evil rejected.
Hence is *Hope* a[nd] Fear
in the desire,
and dislike.
Hence is *Love* a[nd] Joy,
in the Fruition:
But *Anger* and

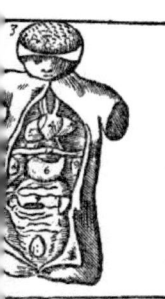

Cartilagines,
Ossa & Viscera.

Cute, 1. detractâ,
Caro, 2. apparet,
ion continuâ
nassâ,
ed distributa,
anquam in
arcimina,
quos vocant *Mus-*
ulos,
quorum numer-
intur
quadringenti
quinque,
canales Spiritu-
m,
d movendum
Aembra.

iscera sunt
Aembra interna:

Jt in Capite,
Cerebrum, 3.
ircumdatum
Cranio, &
Pericranio.

n Pectore, Cor,

bvolutum
Pericardio,
& Pulmo, 5.
espirans.

n Ventre,

the *Stomach*, 6.
and the *Guts*, 7.
covered with a
Caul.
The *Liver*, 8.
and in the left side
opposite
against it, the *Milt*,
9.
the two *Kidneys*,
10.
and the *Bladder*,
11.
The Breast
is divided from the
Belly
by a thick Mem-
brane,
which is called the
Mid-riff, 12.

XLI.

The Chanels and Bones.

Canales & Ossa.

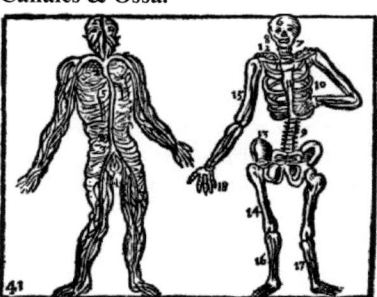

The Chanels of the
Body are
51 the *Veins*, car-
rying
the Blood from the
Liver;
The *Arteries* (car-
rying)
Heart and *Life*
from the
Heat;
The *Nerves* (carry-
ing)
Sense and Motion
throughout the
Body from
the *Brain.*
You shall find
these three, 1.

Ventriculus, 6.
& *Intestina*, 7.
obducta *Omento.*
Jecur, (Hepar) 8.
& à sinistro op-
positus
ei *Lien,* 9.
duo *Renes,* 10.
cum *Vesica,* 11.

Pectus
dividitur à Ventre
crassâ Mem-
branâ,
quæ vocatur *Di-*
aphragma, 12.

Canales Corporis
sunt
Venæ deferentes
Sanguinem ex
Hepate;

Arteriæ,
Calorem & Vitam
è
Corde;

Nervi,
Sensum et Mo-
tum,
per Corpus a
Cerebro.

Invenies hæc tria,
1.

everywhere joined
together.
Besides, from the
Mouth
into the Stomach
is
the *Gullet,* 2. the
way of the meat
and drink;
and by it to the
Lights, the
Wezand, 5. for
breathing;
from the Stomach
to the Anus
is a great *Intestine,*
3.
to purge out the
Ordure;
from the Liver to
the
Bladder, the
Ureter, 4.
for making water.
The *Bones* are
in the Head, the
Skull, 6.
the two *Cheek-*
bones, 7.
with thirty-two
Teeth, 8.
Then the *Back-*
bone, 9.
the Pillar of the
Body,
consisting of thir-
ty-four
turning *Joints,* that
the
Body may bend it
self.
The *Ribs,* 10.
whereof
there are twenty-
four.
The *Breast-bone,*
11.
the two *Shoulder-*
blades, 12.
the *Buttock-bone,*
13.
the *bigger Bone*
in the Arm, 15.
and

ubique sociata.

Porrò, ab Ore
in Ventriculum
Gula, 2.
via cibi ac potus;
& juxta hanc, ad
Pulmonem
Guttur, 5. pro
respiratione;
à ventriculo ad
Anum
Colon, 3.
ad excernendum
Stercus;
ab Hepate ad
Vesicam, *Ureter,*
4.
reddendæ urinæ.

Ossa sunt
in Capite, *Cal-*
varia, 6.
duæ *Maxillæ,* 7.
cum XXXII.
Dentibus, 8.

Tum, *Spina dor-*
si, 9.
columna Cor-
poris,
constans ex
XXXIV.
Vertebris, ut
Corpus queat
flectere se

Costæ, 10.
quarum
viginti quatuor.

Os Pectoris, 11.
duæ *Scapulæ,* 12.
Os sessibuli, 13.
Lacerti, 15.
& *Ulna.*

XXXVIII.

The Outward Parts of a Man.

Membra Hominis Externa.

The *Head*, 1. is above,
the *Feet*, 20. below.
46 the fore part of the Neck
(which ends at the *Arm-holes*, 2.)
is the *Throat*, 3.
the hinder part, the *Crag*, 4.

The *Breast*, 5. is before;
the *back*, 6. behind;
Women have in it two *Dugs*, 7.
with *Nipples*,

Under the Breast is the *Belly*, 9.
in the middle of it the *Navel*, 10.
underneath the *Groyn*, 11.
and the *privities*.
The *Shoulder-blades*, 12. are behind the back,
on which the *Shoulders* depend, 13.
on these the *Arms*, 14.
with the *Elbow*, 15. and then
on either side the *Hands*,
the *right*, 8. and the *left*, 16.
The *Loyns*

Caput, 1. est supra,
infra *Pedes*, 20.
Anterior pars Colli
(quod desit in *Axillas*, 2.)
est *Jugulum*, 3.
posterior *Cervix*, 4.

Pectus, 5. est ante;
Dorsum, 6. retro;
Fœminis sunt in illo
binæ *Mammæ*, 7.
cum *Papillis*.

Sub pectore est *Venter*, 9.
in ejus medio,
Umbelicus, 10.
subtus *Inguen*, 11.
& *pudenda*.
Scapulæ, 12.
sunt a tergo,
à quibus pendent *humeri*, 13.
ab his *Brachia*, 14.
cum *Cubito*, 15.
inde
ad utrumque Latus, *Manus*,
Dextera, 8. &
Sinistra, 16.

Lumbi, 17.

are next the Shoulders,
with the *Hips*, 18.
and in the *Breech*,
the *Buttocks*, 19.

These make the *Foot*;
the *Thigh*, 21. then
the *Leg*, 23.
(the *Knee*, being betwixt them, 22.)
in which is the *Calf*, 24.
with the *Shin*, 25.
then the *Ankles*, 26.
the *Heel*, 27.
and the *Sole*, 28.
in the very end.
the great *Toe*, 29.
with four (other) *Toes*.
47

excipiunt *Humeros*,
cum *Coxis*, 18.
& *in Podice*, (culo)
Nates, 19.

Absolvunt Pedem;
Femur, 21. tum
Crus, 23.
(*Genu*, 22. intermedio.)
in quo *Sura*, 24.
cum *Tilia*, 25.
abhinc *Tali*, 26.
Calx, (Calcaneum) 27.
& *Solum*, 28.
in extremo
Hallux, 29.
cum quatuor *Digitis*.

XXXIX.

The Head and the Hand.

Caput & Manus.

In the *Head* are
the *Hair*, 1.
(which is combed with a *Comb*, 2.)
two *Ears*, 3.
the *Temples*, 4.
and the *Face*, 5.
In the Face are
the *Fore-head*, 6.
both the *Eyes*, 7.
the *Nose*, 8.
(with two *Nostrils*)
the *Mouth*, 9.
the *Cheeks*, 10.
and the *Chin*, 13.

In *Capite* sunt
Capillus, 1.
(qui pectitur *Pectine*, 2.)
Aures, 3. binæ,
& *Tempora*, 4.
Facies, 5.
In facie sunt
Frons, 6.
Oculus, 7.
uterque,
Nasus, 8.
(cum duabus *Naribus*)
Os, 9.
Genæ, (Malæ) 10.

The *Mouth* is fenced
with a *Mustacho*, 11.
and *Lips*, 12.
48 A *Tongue* and a *Palate*,
and *Teeth*, 16.
in the *Cheek-bone*
A Man's Chin
is covered with a *Beard*, 14.
and the Eye
(in which is the *White*
and the *Apple*)
with *eye-lids*,
and an *eye-brow*, 15.

The *Hand* being closed
is a *Fist*, 17.
being open is a *Palm*, 18.
in the midst, is the *hollow*, 19.
of the Hand,
the extremity is the *Thumb*, 20.
with four *Fingers*
the *Fore-finger*, 21
the *Middle-finger*, 22.
the *Ring-finger*, 23
and the *Little-finger*, 24

In every one are three *joynts*, a. b.
and as many *knuckles*, d. e. f.
with a *Nail*, 25.

49

XL.

The Flesh and Bones

Caro & Viscera.

In the *Body* are the *Skin*
with the *Membranes*,
the *Flesh* with the *Muscles*,

longitudinem viri.
Silurus, 8. bucculentus, major illo est:

Sed maximus *Antaseus* (Huso,) 9.
Apuæ, 10. natantes gregatim, sunt minutissimæ.
Alii hujus generis sunt
Perca, Alburnus, Mullus, (Barbus) *Thymallus, Trutta,*
Gobius, Tinca, 11.
Cancer, 12. tegitur crusta, habetque *chelas*, & graditur porro & retrò.

Hirudo, 13. sugit sanguinem.

ish.
chæ.
alæna, (Cetus)
aximus Piscium arinorum.
elphinus, 2.
elocissimus.
aia, 3.

the most monstrous.
Others are the *Lamprel*, 4.
the *Salmon*, or the *Lax*, 5.
There are also fish that flie, 6.
Add *Herrings*, 7. which are brought pickled,
and *Place*, 8. and *Cods*, 9. which are brought dry;
and the Sea monsters,
the *Seal*. 10.
and the *Sea-horse*, &c.
Shell-fish, 11. have Shells.
The *Oyster*, 12. affordeth sweet meat.
The *Purple-fish*, 13. purple;
The others, Pearls, 14.

XXXVI.
Man.
Homo.

Adam, 1. the first Man,
44 was made by God
after his own Image the sixth day of the Creation,
of a lump of Earth.

And *Eve*, 2. the first Woman,

monstrosissimus.
Alii sunt *Murænula*, 4.
Salmo, (Esox) 5.

Dantur etiam volatiles, 6.
Adde *Haleces*, 7. qui salsi,
& *Passeres*, 8.
cum *Asellis*, 9.
qui adferuntur arefacti;
& monstra marina,
Phocam, 10.
Hippopotamum, &c.

Concha, 11. habet testas,
Ostrea, 12. dat sapidam carnem.
Murex, 13. purpuram;
Alii, 14. Margaritas.

Adamus, 1. primus Homo, formatus est a Deo
ad Imaginem suam
sextâ die Creationis,
e Gleba Terræ.

Et *Eva*, 2. prima mulier,

was made of the Rib of the Man.
These, being tempted by the *Devil* under the shape of a *Serpent*, 3.
when they had eaten of
the fruit of the *forbidden Tree*, 4.
were condemned, 5. to misery and death, with all their posterity,
and cast out of *Paradise*, 6.

XXXVII.
The Seven Ages of Man.
Septem Ætates Hominis.

A *Man* is first an *Infant*, 1.
45 then a *Boy*, 2.
then a *Youth*, 3.
then a *Young-man*, 4.
then a *Man*, 5.
after that an *Elderly-man*, 6.
and at last, a *decrepid old man*, 7.
So also in the other *Sex*,
there are, a *Girl*, 8.
A *Damosel*, 9. a *Maid*, 10.
A *Woman*, 11.
an *elderly Woman*, 12. and
a *decrepid old Woman*, 13.

formata est e costâ viri.
Hi, seducti à *Diabolo* sub specie *Serpentis*, 3.
cum comederent de
fructu *vetitæ arboris*, 4.
damnati sunt, 5.
ad miseriam & mortem,
cum omni posteritate sua,
& ejecti e *Paradiso* 6.

Homo est primum *Infans*, 1.
deinde *Puer*, 2.
tum *Adolescens*, 3.
inde *Juvenis*, 4.
posteà *Vir*, 5.
dehinc *Senex*, 6.
tandem *Silicernium*, 7.
Sic etiam in altero *Sexu*,
sunt, *Pupa*, 8.
Puella, 9. *Virgo*, 10.
Mulier, 11.
Vetula, 12.
Anus decrepita, 13.

38 The *Asp*, 4. in the fields.	*Aspis*, 4. in campis.	The *Book-worm*, 7. a Book.	*Blatta*, 7. Librum.	Goose, and a scaly tail to swim.
The *Boa*, (or Mild-snake) 5. in Houses.	*Boa*, 5. in Domibus.	*Maggots*, 8. Flesh and Cheese.	*Termites*, 8. carnem & caseum.	The *Otter*, 3. The croaking *Frog*, 4. with the *Toad*.
The *Slow-worm*, 6. is blind.	*Cæcilia*, 6. est cœca.	*Hand-worms*, the Hair.	*Acari*, Capillum.	The *Tortoise*, 5. covered above and beneath with shells, as with a target. 41
The *Lizzard*, 7. and the *Salamander*, 8. (that liveth long in fire) have feet.	*Lacerta*, 7. *Salamandra*, 8. (in igne vivax,) habent pedes.	The skipping *Flea*, 9. the *Lowse*, 10. and the stinking *Wall-louse*, 11. bite us.	Saltans *Pulex*, 9. *Pediculus*, 10. fœtans *Cimex*, 11. mordent nos.	
The *Dragon*, 9. a winged Serpent, killeth with his Breath.	*Draco*, 9. *Serpens alatus*, necat halitu.	The *Tike*, 12. is a blood-sucker.	*Ricinus*, 12. sanguisugus est.	**XXXIV.** **River Fish and P** **Pisces Fluviatiles**
The *Basilisk*, 10. with his Eyes;	*Basiliscus*, 10. Oculis;	The *Silk-worm*, 13. maketh silk.	*Bombyx*, 13. facit sericum.	
And the *Scorpion*, 11. with his poysonous tail.	*Scorpio*, 11. venenatâ caudâ.	The *Pismire*, 14. is painful.	*Formica*, 14. est laboriosa.	
		The *Spider*, 15. weaveth a Cobweb, nets for flies.	*Aranea*, 15. texit Araneum, retia muscis.	
XXXII. **Crawling-Vermin.** **Insecta repentia.**		The *Snail*, 16. carrieth about her Snail-horn. 40	*Cochlea*, 16. circumfert testam.	A *Fish* hath *Fins*, 1. with which it swimmeth, and *Gills*, 2. by which it taketh breath, and *Prickles* instead of bones: besides the *Male* hath a *Milt*, and the *Female* a *Row*. Some have *Scales* as the *Carp*, 3. and the *Luce* or *Pike*, 4. Some are sleek as the *Eel*, 5. and the *Lamprey* 6. The *Sturgeon*, 7. having a sharp snout, groweth beyond

Worms gnaw *things*.	*Vermes*, rodunt res.
39 The *Earth-worm*, 1. the Earth.	*Lumbricus*, 1. terram.
The *Caterpillar*, 2. the Plant.	*Eruca*, 2. plantam.
The *Grashopper*, 3. the Fruits.	*Cicada*, 3. Fruges.
The *Mite*, 4. the Corn.	*Curculio*, 4. Frumenta.
The *Timber-worm*, 5. Wood.	*Teredo*, (cossis) 5. Ligna.
The *Moth*, 6. a garment.	*Tinea*, 6. vestem.

XXXIII.

Creatures that live as well by Water as by Land.

Amphibia.

Creatures that live by land and by water, are	Viventia in terrâ & aquâ, sunt
The *Crocodile*, 1. a cruel and preying Beast of the River *Nilus*;	*Crocodilus*, 1. immanis & prædatrix bestia Nili fluminis;
The *Castor* or *Beaver*, 2. having feet like a	*Castor*, (Fiber) 2. habens pedes anserinos

Asinus, 1.
& Mulus, 2.
gestant Onera.
Equus, 3.
(quam Juba, 4.
ornat)
gestat nos ipsos.
Camelus, 5.
gestat Mercatorem
cum mercibus suis.
Elephas, (Barrus) 6.
attrahit pabulum
Proboscide, 7.
Habet duos
dentes, 8.
prominentes,
& potest portare
etiam triginta
viros.

being bigger than an Horse (whose back is impenetrable) hath knaggy horns as also the *Hart*, 4.
but the *Roe*, 5. and the *Hind-calf*, almost none.
The *Stone-back*, 6. huge great ones.
The *Wild-goat*, 7. hath very little ones, by which she hangeth her self on a Rock.
36 The *Unicorn*, 8. hath but one, but that a precious one.
The *Boar*, 9. assaileth one with his tushes.
The *Hare*, 10. is fearful.
The *Cony*, 11. diggeth the Earth.
As also the *Mole*, 12. which maketh hillocks.

major equo
(cujus tergus est
impenetrabilis)
habet ramosa cornua:
ut & *Cervus*, 4.

Sed *Caprea*, 5.
cum
Hinnulo, ferè nulla.
Capricornus, 6.
prægrandia;

Rupicapra, 7.
minuta,
quibus suspendit
se ad rupem.

Monoceros, 8.
habet unum,
sed pretiosum.

Aper, 9.
grassatur dentibus.

Lepus, 10. pavet.
Cuniculus, 11.
perfodit terram;

Ut & *Talpa*, 12.
quæ facit grumos.

XXX.

Wild-Beasts.

Feræ **Bestiæ**.

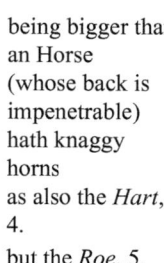

Wild Beasts have

Bestiæ habent

sharp paws, and teeth,
and are flesh eaters.

As the *Lyon*, 1.
the King of four-footed Beasts,
having a mane;
with the *Lioness*.
The spotted *Panther*, 2.

37 The *Tyger*, 3.
the cruellest of all.

The Shaggy *Bear*, 4.
The ravenous *Wolf*, 5.
The quick sighted *Ounce*, 6.
The tayled *fox*, 7.
the craftiest of all.

The *Hedge-hog*, 8.
is prickly.
The *Badger*, 9.
delighteth in holes.

acutos ungues,
& dentes,
suntque carnivoræ.

Ut *Leo*, 1.
Rex quadrupedum,
jubatus;
cum *Leænâ*.
Maculosus,
Pardo
(Panthera) 2.

Tygris, 3.
immanissima omnium.

Villosus *Ursus*, 4.
Rapax *Lupus*, 5.
Lynx, 6. visu pollens,
Caudata *Vulpes*, 7.
astutissima omnium.

Erinaceus, 8.
est aculeatus.
Melis, 9.
gaudet latebris.

XXXI.

Serpents and Creeping things.

Serpentes & Reptilia.

Snakes creep
by winding themselves;
The *Adder*, 1.
in the wood;
The *Water-snake*, 2.
in the water;

The *Viper*, 3.
amongst great stones.

Angues repunt
sinuando se;
Coluber, 1.
in Sylvâ.
Natrix, (hydra) 2.
in Aquâ;

Vipera, 3.
in saxis;

greater Birds.

XXIV.

Water-Fowl.

Aves Aquaticæ.

The white *Swan*, 1.	*Oler*, 1. can-
the *Goose*, 2.	didus.
and the *Duck*, 3.	*Anser*, 2.
swim up and down.	& *Anas*, 3.
	natant.
The *Cormorant*, 4.	*Mergus*, 4.
diveth.	se mergit.
Add to these the wa-	Adde his *Fuli-*
ter-hen,	*cam*,
and the *Pelican*, &c.,	*Pelecanum*,
10.	&c., 10.
31 The *Osprey*, 5	*Haliæetus*, 5.
and the *Sea-mew*, 6.	& *Gavia*, 6.
flying downwards	devolantes,
use to catch Fish,	captant pisces,
but the *Heron*, 7.	sed *Ardea*, 7.
standing on the	stans in ripis.
Banks.	
The *Bittern*, 8. put-	*Butio*, 8. inferit
teth	rostrum aquæ,
his Bill in the water,	&
and	mugit ut bos.
belloweth like an	
Ox.	
The *Water-wagtail*,	*Motacilla*, 9.
9.	motat caudam.
waggeth the tail.	

XXV.

Flying Vermin.

Insecta volantia.

The *Bee*, 1. maketh	*Apis*, 1. facit
honey	mel
which the *Drone*, 2.	quod *Fucus*, 2.
devoureth.	depascit
The *Wasp*, 3.	*Vespa*, 3.
and the *Hornet*, 4.	& *Crabro*, 4.
molest with a sting;	infestant oculeo;

and the *Gad-Bee*	& *Oestrum*
(or Breese), 5.	(Asilus), 5.
especially *Cattel*;	imprimis *pecus*,
32 but the *Fly*, 6.	autem *Musca*, 6.
and the *Gnat*, 7. us.	& *Culex*, 7. nos.
The *Cricket*, 8.	*Gryllus*, 8. can-
singeth.	tillat.
The *Butterfly*, 9. is	*Papillio*, 9. est
a	alata *Eruca*.
winged *Caterpillar*.	
The *Beetle*, 10.	*Scarabæus*, 10.
covereth	tegit
her wings with	alas *vaginis*.
Cases.	
The *Glow-worm*,	*Cicindela*
11.	[Lampyris], 11.
shineth by night.	nitet noctu.

XXVI.

Four-Footed Beasts: and First those about the House.

Quadrupeda: & primum Domestica.

The *Dog*, 1.	*Canis*, 1.
with the *Whelp*, 2.	cum *Catello*, 2.
is keeper of the	est custos Domûs.
House.	
The *Cat*, 3.	*Felis* (Catus) 3.
33 riddeth the	purgat domum
House	à *Muribus*, 4.
of *Mice*, 4.	quod etiam
which also	*Muscipula*, 5. fac-
a *Mouse-trap*, 5.	it.
doth.	
A *Squirrel*, 6.	*Sciurus*, 6.
The *Ape*, 7.	*Simia*, 7.

and the *Monkey*, 8.
are kept at home for delight.
The *Dormouse*, 9. and
other greater Mice, 10
as, the *Weesel*, the *Marten*,
and the *Ferret*, trouble the House.

XXVII.

Herd-Cattle.

Pecora.

The *Bull*, 1. the *Cow*, 2.
and the *Calf*, 3.
are covered with hair.
The *Ram*, the *Weather*, 4.
the *Ewe*, 5. and the *Lamb*, 6.
bear wool.
34 The *He-goat*, the *Gelt-goat*, 7.
with the *She-goat* 8.
and *Kid*, 9. have *shag-hair* and *beards*.
The *Hog*, the *Sow* 10.
and the *Pigs*, 11. have *bristles*
but not *horns*;
but also *cloven feet* as those others (have.)

gride, 9.

Formosus *Pavo*, 10.
superbit pennis.

Ciconia, 11.
nidificat
in tecto.

Hirundo, 12.
Passer, 13.
Pica, 14.
Monedula, 15.
& *Vespertilio*, 16.
(Mus alatus)
volitant circa Domus.

Luscinia
(*Philomela*), 1.
cantat suavissime
omnium.
Alauda, 2. cantillat
volitans in aere;

Coturnix, 3.
sedens humi;

Cæteræ, in ramis
arborum, 4.
ut *Luteola* peregrina.
Fringilla,
Carduelis,
Acanthis,

the *Linnet*,
the little *Titmouse*,
the *Wood-wall*,
the *Robin-redbreast*,
the *Hedge-sparrow*, &c.
The party colour'd
Parret, 5.
the *Black-bird*, 6.
the *Stare*, 7.
with the *Mag-pie*
and the *Jay*, learn
28 to frame men's
words.

A great many are
wont
to be shut in
Cages, 8.

XXII.

Birds that haunt the Fields and Woods.

Aves Campestres & Sylvestres

The *Ostrich*, 1.
is the greatest
Bird.
The *Wren*, 2.
is the least.

The *Owl*, 3.
is the most despicable.
The *Whoopoo*, 4.
is the most nasty,
for it eateth dung.

The *Bird of Paradise*, 5.
is very rare.

The *Pheasant*, 6.
the *Bustard*, 7.
29 the deaf wild

Linaria,
parvus *Parus*,
Galgulus,
Rubecula,
Curruca, &c.

Discolor *Psittacus*, 5.
Merula, 6.
Sturnus, 7.
cum *Pica*,
& *Monedula*,
discunt
humanas voces
formare

Pleræque solent
includi *Caveis*, 8.

Struthio, 1.
ales est maximus.

Regulus, 2.
(Trochilus)
minimus.
Noctua, 3.
despicatissimus.
Upupa, 4.
sordidissimus,
vescitur enim
stercoribus.

Manucodiata, 5.
rarissimus.

Phasianus, 6.
Tarda (Otis), 7.
surdus, *Tetrao*, 8.

Peacock, 8.
the *Moor-hen*, 9.
the *Partrige*, 10.
the *Woodcock*, 11.
and the *Thrush*, 12.
are counted Dainties.
Among the rest,
the best are,
the watchful
Crane, 13.
the mournful *Turtle*, 14.
the *Cuckow*, 15.
the *Stock-dove*,
the *Speight*,
the *Jay*,
the *Crow*, &c., 16.

XXIII.

Ravenous Birds.

Aves Rapaces.

The *Eagle*, 1.
the King of Birds
looketh upon the
Sun.
The *Vulture*, 2.
and the *Raven*, 3.
30 feed upon *Carrion*.

The *Kite*, 4. pursueth
Chickens.

The *Falcon*, 5.
the *Hobbie*, 6.
and the *Hawk*, 7.
catch at little
Birds.
The *Gerfalcon*, 8.
catcheth
Pigeons and

Attagen, 9.
Perdix, 10.
Gallinago (Rusticola), 11.
& *Turdus*, 12.
habentur in
deliciis.

Inter reliquas,
potissimæ sunt,
Grus 13. pervigil.

Turtur, 14.
gemens.
Cuculus, 15.
Palumbes,
Picus,
Garrulus,
Cornix, &c., 16.

Aquila, 1.
Rex Avium,
intuetur Solem.

Vultur, 2.
& *Corvus*, 3.
pascuntur morticinis,
[cadaveribus.]

Milvus, 4. insectatur
pullos gallinaceos.

Falco, 5.
Nisus, 6.
& *Accipiter*, 7.
captant aviculas.

Astur, 8. captat
columbas & aves
majores.

in which the *Ear* hath *awnes*, or else it is without awnes, and it nourisheth the *Corn* in the *Husk*.	ut, *Triticum*, 1. *Siligo*, 2. *Hordeum*, 3. in quibus *Spica* habet *Aristas*, aut est mutica, fovetque *grana* in *gluma*.	bearing *Cats-tails*, and the *Reed*, 3. which is knotty and hollow within.	ferens *Typhos*, & *Arundo*, 3. nodosa et cava intus.	flyeth with *Wings* 3. hath two *Pinions*, as many *Feet*, 5. a *Tail*, 6. and a *Bill*, 7.
		Elsewhere, 4. 24 the *Rose*, the *Bastard-Corinths*, the *Elder*, the *Juniper*.	Alibi, 4. *Rosa*, *Ribes*, *Sambucus*, *Juniperus*.	The *Shee*, 8. layeth Eggs, 10. in a nest, 9. and sitting upon them, hatcheth *young ones*, 11.
Some instead of an ear, have a *rizom* (or plume) containing the corn by bunches, as *Oats*, 4. *Millet*, 5. *Turkey-wheat*, 6.	Quædam pro Spica, habent *Paniculam*, continentem grana fasciatim, ut, *Avena*, 4. *Milium*, 5. *Frumentum Saracenicum*, 6.	Also the *Vine*, 5. which putteth forth *branches*, 6. and these *tendrels*, 7. *Vine-leaves*, 8. and Bunches of grapes, 9. on the stock whereof hang *Grapes*, which contain *Grape-stones*.	Item *Vitis*, 5. quæ emittit *Palmites*, 6. et hi *Capreolos*, 7. *Pampinos*, 8. et *Racemos*, 9. quorum Scapo pendent *Uvæ*, continentes *Acinos*.	An *Egg* is cover'd with a *Shell*, 12. under which is the *White*, 13. in this the *Yolk*, 14.
23 *Pulse* have *Cods*, which enclose the corns in two *Shales*, as *Pease*, 7. *Beans*, 8. *Vetches*, 9. and those that are less than these *Lentils* and *Urles* (or Tares).	*Legumina* habent *Siliquas*, quæ includunt grana valvulis, ut, *Pisum*, 7. *Fabæ*, 8. *Vicia*, 9. & minores his *Lentes* & *Cicera*.			XX. **Tame Fowls.** **Aves Domesticæ.**
XVIII. **Shrubs.** **Frutices.**		**XIX.** **Living-Creatures: and First, Birds.** **Animalia: & primum, Aves**		

A plant being greater, and harder than an herb, is called a *Shrub*: such as are In Banks and Ponds, the *Rush*, 1. the *Bulrush*, 2. or Cane without knots	Planta major & durior herba, dicitur *Frutex*: ut sunt In ripis & stagnis, *Juncus*, 1. *Scirpus*, 2. [Canna] enodis	A *living Creature* liveth, perceiveth, moveth it self; is born, dieth, is nourished, and groweth: standeth, or sitteth, or lieth, or goeth. 25 A *Bird*, (here the King's *Fisher*, 1.* making her nest in the Sea.) is covered with *Feathers*, 2.	*Animal* vivit, sentit, movet se; nascitur, moritur, nutritur, & crescit; stat, aut sedet, aut cubat, aut graditur. *Avis*, (hic *Halcyon*, 1. in mari nidulans.) tegitur *Plumis*, 2. volat *Pennis*, 3.	The *Cock*, 1. (which croweth in the Morning.) 26 hath a *Comb*, and *Spurs*, 3. being gelded, he called a *Capon*, and is crammed in a *Coop*, 4. A *Hen*, 5. scrapeth the *Dunghil*, and picketh up Corns: as also the *Pigeons*, 6. (which are brought up in a *Pigeon-house*,

Pyrum, 2. & *Ficus*, 3.
sunt oblonga.
Cerasum, 4.
pendet longo *Pediolo*.
Prunum, 5.
& *Persicum*, 6.
breviori.
Morum, 7.
brevissimo.
Nux Juglans, 8.
Avellana, 9.
& *Castanea*, 10.
involuta sunt
Cortici
& *Putamini*.
Steriles arbores
sunt 11.
*Abies, Alnus,
Betula, Cupressus,
Fagus, Fraxinus,
Salix, Tilia,*
&c. sed
pleræque
umbriferæ.
At *Juniperus*,
12.
& *Laurus*, 13.
ferunt *Baccas*.
Pinus, 14. *Strobilos*.
Quercus, 15.
Glandes & Gallas.

nter flores
otissimi,

the most noted,
In the beginning
of the Spring are
the *Violet*, 1. the
Crow-toes, 2.
the *Daffodil*, 3.
Then the *Lillies*, 4.
white and yellow
and blew, 5.
and the *Rose*, 6.
and the
Clove-gilliflowers,
7. &c.
Of these *Garlands*,
8.
and *Nosegays*, 9.
are tyed round
with twigs.
There are added
also
sweet herbs, 10.
as *Marjoram,
Flower gentle,
Rue,
Lavender,
Rosemary,*
21 *Hysop, Spike,
Basil, Sage,
Mints,* &c.

Amongst Fieldflowers, 11.
the most noted are
the *May-lillie,
Germander,* the
*Blew-Bottle,
Chamomel,* &c.

And amongst
Herbs,
*Trefoil,
Wormwood, Sorrel,*
the *Nettle,* &c.

Primo vere,
Viola, 1. *Hyacinthus*, 2.
Narcissus, 3.

Tum *Lilia*, 4.
alba & lutea,
& cœrulea, 5.
tandem *Rosa*, 6.
&
Caryophillum, 7.
&c.
Ex his *Serta*, 8.
& *Serviæ*, 9.
vientur.

Adduntur etiam
Herbæ odoratæ,
10.
ut *Amaracus,
Amaranthus, Ruta,
Lavendula,
Rosmarinus,*
(Libanotis),
*Hyposus, Nard,
Ocymum, Salvia,
Menta,* &c.

Inter Campestres
Flores, 11.
notissimi sunt
*Lilium Convallium,
Chamædrys,
Cyanus,
Chamæmelum,*
&c.

Et Herbæ,
Cytisus (Trifolium)
*Absinthium, Acetosa,
Urtica,* &c.

The *Tulip*, 12.
is the grace of
flowers,
but affording no
smell.

Tulipa, 12.
est decus Florum,
sed expers
odoris.

XVI.

Potherbs.

Olera.

Pot-herbs
grow in Gardens,
as *Lettice*, 1.
Colewort, 2.
Onions, 3. 22 *Garlick*, 4.
Gourd, 5.
The *Parsnep*, 6.
The *Turnep*, 7.
The *Radish*, 8.
Horse-radish, 9.
Parsly, 10.
Cucumbers, 11.
and *Pompions*, 12.

Olera
nascuntur in
hortis,
ut *Lactuca*, 1.
Brassica, 2.
Cepa, 3. *Allium*, 4.
Cucurbita, 5.
Siser, 6.
Rapa, 7.
Raphanus minor, 8.
Raphanus major, 9.
Petroselinum,
10.
Cucumeres, 11.
Pepones, 12.

XVII.

Corn.

Fruges.

Some *Corn* grows
upon a *straw*,
parted by *knots*,
as *Wheat*, 1.
Rie, 2. *Barley*, 3.

Frumenta quædam crescunt
super *culmum*,
distinctum *geniculis*,

XI.

Metals.

Metalla.

Lead, 1. is soft, and heavy.	Plumbum, 1. est molle & grave.
Iron, 2. is hard, and Steel, 3. harder.	Ferrum, 2. est durum, & Calybs, 3. durior.
They make Tankards (or Cans), 4. of Tin.	Faciunt Cantharos, 4. e Stanno.
Kettles, 5. of Copper,	Ahena, 5. e Cupro,
Candlesticks, 6. of Latin,	Candelabra, 6. ex Orichalco,
Dollers, 7. of Silver,	Thaleros, 7. ex Argento,
Ducats and Crown-pieces, 8. of Gold.	Scutatos et Coronatos, 8. Ex Auro.
Quick-silver is always liquid, and eateth thorow Metals.	Argentum Vivum, semper liquet, & corrodit Metalla.

16

XII.

Stones.

Lapides.

Sand, 1. and Gravel, 2. is Stone broken into bits.	Arena, 1. & Sabulum, 2. est Lapis comminutus.
A great Stone, 3. is a piece of a Rock (or Crag) 4.	Saxum, 3. est pars Petræ (Cautis) 4.
A Whetstone, 5. a Flint, 6. a Marble, 7. &c. are ordinary Stones.	Cos, 5. Silex, 6. Marmor, 7. &c. sunt obscuri Lapides.
A Load-stone, 8. draweth Iron to it.	Magnes, 8. adtrahit ferrum.
Jewels, 9. are clear Stones, as	Gemmæ, 9. sunt pellucidi Lapilli,
The Diamond white	ut Adamas candidus,
The Ruby red,	Rubinus rubeus,
The Sapphire blue,	Sapphirus cæruleus,
The Emerald green,	Smaragdus viridis,
The Jacinth yellow, &c.	Hyacynthus luteus, &c.
And they glister being cut into corners.	et micant angulati.
Pearls and Unions, 10. grow in Shell-fish.	Margaritæ & Uniones, 10. crescunt in Conchis.
17 Corals, 11. in a Sea-shrub.	Corallia, 11. in Marinâ arbusculâ.
Amber, 12. is gathered from the Sea.	Succinum, 12. colligitur è mari.
Glass, 13. is like Chrystal.	Vitrum, 13. simile est Chrystallo.

XIII.

Tree.

Arbor.

A Plant, 1. groweth from a Seed.	Planta, 1. procrescit e Semine.
A plant waxeth to a Shoot, 2.	Planta abit in Fruticem, 2.
A Shoot to a Tree, 3.	Frutex in Arborem, 3.

The Root, 4. beareth up the Tree.	
The Body or Stem, 5. riseth from the Root.	
The Stem divideth it self into Boughs, 6. and green Branches, 7. made of Leaves, 8.	
18 The top, 9 is in the height.	
The Stock, 10. is close to the roots.	
A Log, 11 is the body fell'd down without Boughs; having Bark and Rind, 12 Pith and Heart, 13.	
Bird-lime, 14. groweth upon the boughs, which also sweat Gumm, Rosin, Pitch, &c.	

XIV.

Fruits of Trees.

Fructus Arborum

Fruits that have n
shells
are pull'd from
fruit-bearing trees
The Apple, 1. is
round.

qua scatet
Fonte, 1.
efluit
 Torrente, 2.
 anat in *Rivo*, 3.
 at in *Stagno*, 4.
 uit in *Flumine*, 5.
 yratur
 Vortice, 6.
 facit *Paludes*, 7.

lumen habet *Ri-
as*.
 are facit *Littora*,

 inus, 10.
 romontoria, 11.
 sulas, 12.
 eninsulas, 13.
 thmos, 14.
 reta, 15.
 habet *Scopulos*,
 6.

Vapor, 1. ascen-
dit
ex *Aquâ*.

From it a *Cloud*, 2.
is made, and a *white
Mist*, 3.
near the Earth.
Rain, 4.
and a small *Shower*
distilleth out of a
Cloud,
drop by drop.
Which being frozen,
is *Hail*, 5.
half frozen is *Snow*,
6.
being warm is *Mel-
dew*.
In a rainy Cloud,
set over against the
Sun
the *Rainbow*, 7. ap-
peareth.
A *drop* falling into
the water
maketh a *Bubble*, 8.
many *Bubbles* make
froth, 9.

Frozen Water
is called *Ice*, 10.
Dew congealed,
13 is called a *white
Frost*.
Thunder is made of
a brimstone-like
vapour,
which breaking out
of a Cloud,
with *Lightning*, 11.
thundereth and
striketh with light-
ning.

Inde *Nubes*, 2.
fit, et *Nebula*, 3.
prope terram.

Pluvia, 4.
et *Imber*,
stillat e *Nube*,
guttatim.

Quæ gelata,
Grando, 5.
semigelata, *Nix*,
6.
calefacta, *Rubi-
go* est.
In nube plu-
viosâ,
oppositâ soli
Iris, 7. apparet.

Gutta incidens
in aquam,
facit *Bullam*, 8.
multæ *Bullæ*
faciunt
spumam, 9.

Aqua congelata
Glacies, 10.
Ros congelatus,
dicitur *Pruina*.

Tonitru fit ex
Vapore sul-
phureo,
quod erumpens
è Nube
cum *Fulgure*,
11.
tonat &
fulminat.

IX.

The Earth.

Terra.

In the *Earth*
are high *Moun-
tains*, 1.
Deep *Vallies*, 2.
Hills rising, 3.
Hollow *Caves*, 4.
Plain *Fields*, 5.
Shady *Woods*, 6.

In *Terra*
sunt Alti
Montes, 1.
Profundæ *valles*,
2.
Elevati *Colles*, 3.
cavæ *Speluncæ*,
4.
Plani *campi*, 5.
Opacæ *Sylvæ*, 6.

X.

The Fruits of the Earth.

Terræ Fœtus.

A *meadow*,
1. yieldeth *grass*
with *Flowers* and
Herbs,
which being cut
down,
are made *Hay*, 2.
A *Field*, 3. yield-
eth *Corn*,
and *Pot-herbs*, 4.
Mushrooms, 5.
Straw-berries, 6.
Myrtle-trees, &c.
come up in Woods.

Metals, *Stones*,
and
Minerals
grow *under the
earth*.

Pratum, 1.
fert *Gramina*,
cum *Floribus* &
Herbis
quæ defecta
fiunt *Fœnum*, 2.

Arvum, 3. fert
Fruges,
& *Olera*, 4.
Fungi, 5.
Fraga, 6.
Myrtilli, &c.
Proveniunt in
Sylvis.

Metalla, *Lapides*,
Mineralia,
nascuntur sub
terra.

7 Thus the greatest Bodies of the World, the four *Elements*, are full of their own Inhabitants.

7. *Beasts*, 8. and *Men*, 9.

Ita maxima *Corpora Mundi*, quatuor *Elementa*, sunt plena *Habitatoribus* suis.

pos, 7. *Animalia*, 8. *Homines*, 9.

IV.

The Heaven.

Cœlum.

The Heaven, 1. is wheeled about, and encompasseth the *Earth*, 2. standing in the middle.

The *Sun*, 3. wheresoever it is, shineth perpetually, howsoever dark *Clouds*, 4. may take it from us; and causeth by his *Rays*, 5. *Light*, and the Light, *Day*.

On the other side, over against it, is *Darkness*, 6. and thence *Night*.

8 In the Night shineth the *Moon*, 7.

Cœlum, 1. rotatur, & ambit *Terram*, 2. stantem in medio.

Sol, 3. ubi ubi est, fulget perpetuo, ut ut *densa Nubila*, 4. eripiant eum a nobis; facitque suis *Radiis*, 5. *Lucem*, Lux *Diem*.

Ex opposito, sunt *Tenebræ*, 6. inde *Nox*.

Nocte splendet *Luna*, 7.

and the *Stars*, 8. glister and twinkle.

In the Evening, 9. is *Twilight*:

In the *Morning*, 10. the breaking, and dawning of the Day.

V.

Fire.

Ignis.

The *Fire* gloweth, burneth and consumeth to ashes.

A *spark* of it struck out of a *Flint* (or Firestone), 2. by means of a *Steel*, 1. and taken by *Tynder* in a *Tynder-box*, 3. lighteth a *Match*, 4. and after that a *Candle*, 5. 9 or *stick*, 6. and causeth a *flame*, 7. or *blaze*, 8. which catcheth hold of the Houses. *Smoak*, 9. ascendeth therefrom, which, sticking to the *Chimney*, 10. turneth into *Soot*.

& *Stellæ*, 8. micant, scintillant.

Vesperi, 9. est *Crepusculum*:

Manè Aurora, 10. & *Diluculum*.

Ignis ardet, urit, cremat.

Scintilla ejus elisa e *Silice*, (Pyrite) 2. Ope *Chalybis*, 1. et excepta a *Fomite* in *Suscitabulo*, 3. accendit *Sulphuratum*, 4. et inde *Candelam*, 5. vel *Lignum*, 6. et excitat *Flammam*, 7. vel *Incendium*, 8. quod corripit Ædificia.

Fumus, 9. ascendit inde, qui, adhærans *Camino*, 10. abit in *Fuliginem*.

Of a *Fire-brand*, (or burning stick) is made a *Brand*, 11. (or quenched stick). Of a *hot Coal* (red hot piece of a Fire-brand) is made a *Coal*, 12. (or a *dead Cinder*

That which remaineth, is at last *Ashes*, 13 and *Embers* (or hot *Ashes*). 10

VI.

The Air.

Aër.

A cool *Air*, 1. breatheth gently.
The *Wind*, 2 bloweth strongly.
A *Storm*, 3. throweth down Trees.
A *Whirl-wind*, 4. turneth it self in a round compass.
A Wind under Ground, 5. causeth an *Earthquake*.
An Earthquake causeth gapings of the Earth, (and falls of Houses.) 6.

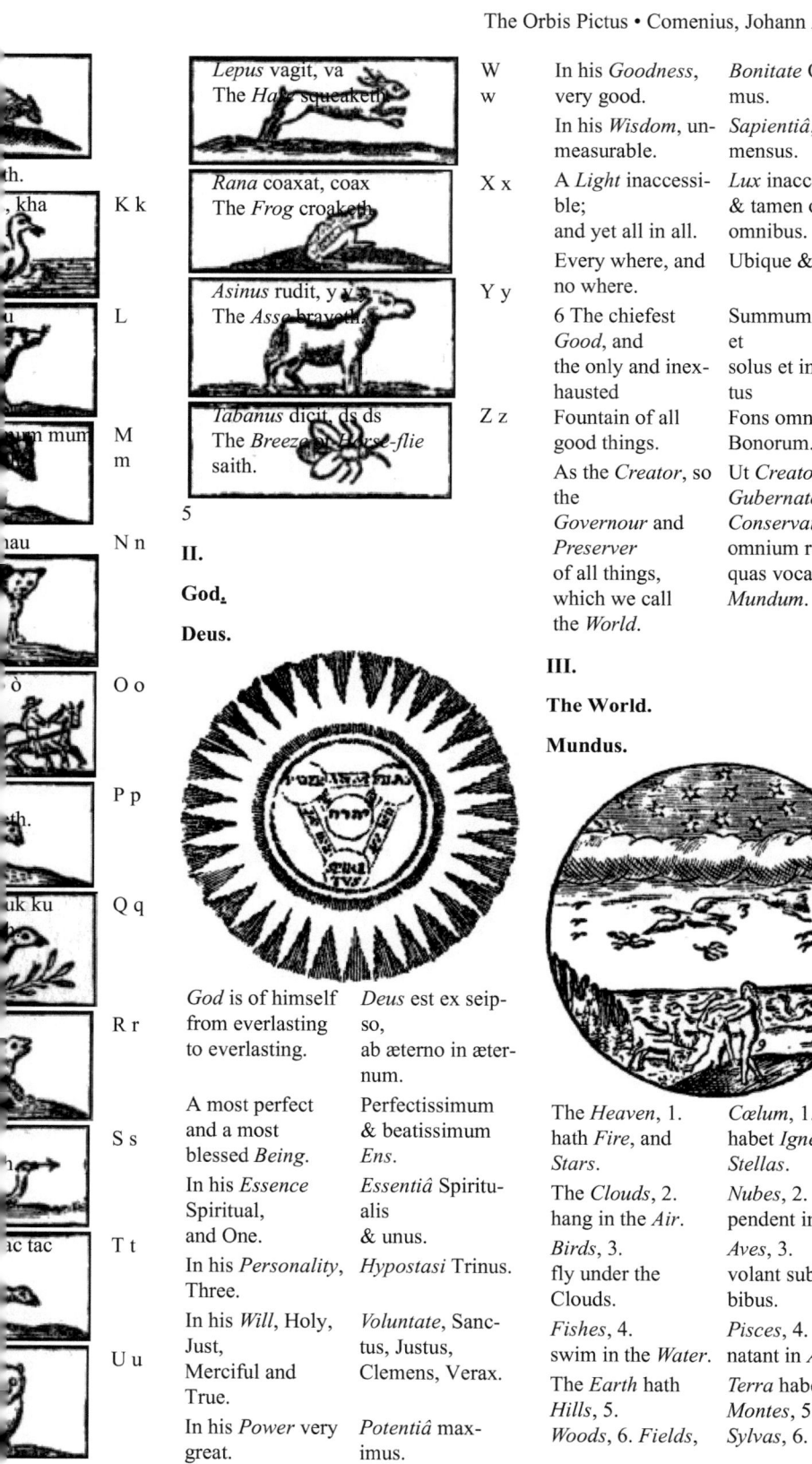

		Lepus vagit, va	W
		The *Hare* squeaketh.	w
	K k		
		Rana coaxat, coax	X x
		The *Frog* croaketh.	
	L	*Asinus* rudit, y	Y y
		The *Ass* brayeth.	
	M m	*Tabanus* dicit, ds ds	Z z
		The *Breeze* or *Horse-flie* saith.	

5

II.

God.

Deus.

	N n		
	O o		
	P p		
	Q q		
	R r		
	S s	*God* is of himself from everlasting to everlasting.	*Deus* est ex seipso, ab æterno in æternum.
		A most perfect and a most blessed *Being*.	Perfectissimum & beatissimum *Ens*.
		In his *Essence* Spiritual, and One.	*Essentiâ* Spiritualis & unus.
	T t	In his *Personality*, Three.	*Hypostasi* Trinus.
		In his *Will*, Holy, Just, Merciful and True.	*Voluntate*, Sanctus, Justus, Clemens, Verax.
	U u	In his *Power* very great.	*Potentiâ* maximus.

In his *Goodness*, very good. — *Bonitate* Optimus.
In his *Wisdom*, unmeasurable. — *Sapientiâ*, immensus.
A *Light* inaccessible; and yet all in all. — *Lux* inaccessa; & tamen omnia in omnibus.
Every where, and no where. — Ubique & nullibi.
6 The chiefest *Good*, and the only and inexhausted Fountain of all good things. — Summum *Bonum*, et solus et inexhaustus Fons omnium Bonorum.
As the *Creator*, so the *Governour* and *Preserver* of all things, which we call the *World*. — Ut *Creator*, ita *Gubernator* et *Conservator* omnium rerum, quas vocamus *Mundum*.

III.

The World.

Mundus.

The *Heaven*, 1. hath *Fire*, and *Stars*. — *Cœlum*, 1. habet *Ignem* & *Stellas*.
The *Clouds*, 2. hang in the *Air*. — *Nubes*, 2. pendent in *Aere*.
Birds, 3. fly under the *Clouds*. — *Aves*, 3. volant sub nubibus.
Fishes, 4. swim in the *Water*. — *Pisces*, 4. natant in *Aqua*.
The *Earth* hath *Hills*, 5. — *Terra* habet *Montes*, 5.
Woods, 6. *Fields*, — *Sylvas*, 6. Cam-

great part of that Heathenish stuff they are tormented with; like the feeding them with hard Nuts, which when they have almost broke their teeth with cracking, they find either deaf or to contain but very rotten and unwholesome Kernels) whilst Things really perfected of the understanding, and useful in every state of Life, are left unregarded, to the Reproach of our Nation, where all other Arts are improved and flourish well, only this of Education of Youth is at a stand; as if that, the good or ill management of which is of the utmost consequence to all, were a thing not worth any Endeavors to improve it, or was already so perfect and well executed that it needed none, when many of the greatest Wisdom and Judgment in several Nations, have with a just indignation endeavor'd to expose it, and to establish a more easy and useful way in its room.

'Tis not easy to say little on so important a subject, but thus much may suffice for the present purpose. The Book has merit enough to recommend it self to those who know how to make a right use of it. It was reckon'd one of the Author's best performances; and besides the many Impressions and Translations it has had in parts beyond Sea, has been several times reprinted here. It was endeavor'd no needless Alterations shou'd be admitted in this Edition, and as little of any as cou'd consist with the design of making it plain and useful; to shun the offence it might give to some; and only the Roman and Italic Character alternately made use of, where transplacing of Words cou'd be avoided.

J. H.
London,
July 13, 1727.

* Mr. Lock's Essay upon Education.
Dr. Tabor's Christian Schoolmaster.
Dr. Ob. Walker of Education.
Mr. Monro's Essay on Education.
—His just Measures of the pious Institutions of Youth, &c.

Orbis Sensualium Pictus,

A World of Things Obvious to the Senses drawn in Pictures.

I.

Invitation.
Invitatio.

The Master and the Boy.	*Magister & Puer.*
M. Come, Boy, learn to be wise.	M. Veni, Puer, disce sapere.
P. What doth this mean, *to be wise*?	P. Quid hoc est, *Sapere*?
M. To understand rightly, 2 to do rightly, and to speak out rightly all that are necessary.	M. Intelligere recte, agere recte, et eloqui recte omnia necessaria.
P. Who will teach me this?	P. Quis docebit me hoc?
M. I, by God's help.	M. Ego, cum DEO.
P. How?	P. Quomodo?
M. I will guide thee thorow all. I will shew thee all.	M. Ducam te per omnia. Ostendam tibi omnia.
I will name thee all.	Nominabo tibi omnia.
P. See, here I am; lead me in the name of God.	P. En, adsum; duc me in nomine DEI.
M. Before all things, thou oughtest to learn the plain *sounds*, of which man's *speech* consisteth; which *living crea-*	M. Ante omnia, debes discere simplices *Sonos* ex quibus *Sermo* humanus constat; quos *Animalia* sciunt *formare*, & tua *Lingua*

tures
know how to make
and thy *Tongue*
knoweth how
to *imitate*, and thy *hand*
can *picture out*.
Afterwards we will go
into the *World*,
and we will view all things.
Here thou hast a lively
and Vocal Alphabet

3
All pictures A-M

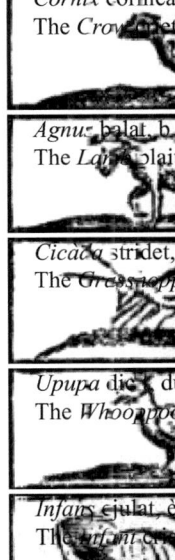

Cornix cornicatur
The *Crow* crieth

Agnus balat,
The *Lamb* blaiteth

Cicada stridet,
The *Grasshopper*

Upupa dicit, du
The *Whooppoo*

Infans ejulat, è
The *Infant*

Ventus flat, fi f
The *Wind*

Anser gingrit,
The *Goose* gag

Os halet
The *Mouth*

Mus mintrit, i

pected an Account should be given of the Reasons for them. 'Tis certain from the Author's Words, that when it was first published, which was in Latin and Hungary, or in Latin and High-Dutch; every where one word answer'd to another over-against it: This might have been observ'd in our English Translation, which wou'd have fully answer'd the design of COMENIUS, and have made the Book much more useful: But Mr. Hoole, (whether out of too much scrupulousness to disturb the Words in some places from the order they were in, or not sufficiently considering the Inconveniences of having the Latin and English so far asunder) has made them so much disagree, that a Boy has sometimes to seek 7 or 8 lines off for the corresponding Word; which is no small trouble to Young Learners who are at first equally unacquainted with all Words, in a Language they are strangers to, except it be such as have Figures of Reference, or are very like in sound; and thus may perhaps, innocently enough join an Adverb in one Tongue, to a Noun in the other; whence may xxix appear the Necessity of the Translation's being exactly literal, and the two Languages fairly answering one another, Line for Line.

If it be objected, such a thing cou'd not be done (considering the difference of the Idioms) without transplacing Words here and there, and putting them into an order which may not perhaps be exactly classical; it ought to be observed, this is design'd for Boys chiefly, or those who are just entering upon the Latin Tongue, to whom every thing ought to be made as plain and familiar as possible, who are not, at their first beginning, to be taught the elegant placing of Latin, nor from such short Sentences as these, but from Discourses where the Periods have a fuller Close. Besides, this way has already taken (according to the Advice of very good Judges,) in some other School-Books of Mr. Hoole's translating, and found to succeed abundantly well.

Such Condescensions as these, to the capacities of young Learners are certainly very reasonable, and wou'd be most agreeable to the Intentions of the Ingenious and worthy Author, and his design to suit whatever he taught, to their manner of apprehending it. Whose Excellency in the art of Education made him so famous all over Europe, as to be solicited by several States and Princes to go and reform the Method of their Schools; and whose works carried that Esteem, that in his own Life-time some part of them were not only translated into 12 of the usual Languages of Europe, but also into the *Arabic*, *Turkish*, *Persian*, and *Mogolic* (the common Tongue of all that part of the *East-Indies*) and since his death, into xxx the *Hebrew*, and some others. Nor did they want their due Encouragement here in *England*, some Years ago; 'till by an indiscreet use of them, and want of a thorow acquaintance with his Method, or unwillingness to part from their old road, they began to be almost quite left off: Yet it were heartily to be wish'd, some Persons of Judgment and Interest, whose Example might have an influence upon others, and bring them into Reputation again, wou'd revive the COMENIAN METHOD, which is no other, than to make our Scholars learn with Delight and chearfulness, and to convey a solid and useful Knowledge of Things, with that of Languages, in an easy, natural and familiar way. *Didactic Works* (as they are now collected into one volume) for a speedy attaining the Knowledge of Things and Words, join'd with the Discourses of Mr. Lock* and 2 or 3 more out of our own Nation, for forming the Mind and settling good Habits, may doubtless be look'd upon to contain the most reasonable, orderly, and completed System of the Art of Education, that can be met with.

Yet, alas! how few are there, who follow the way they have pointed out? tho' every one who seriously considers it, must be convinc'd of the Advantage; and the generality of Schools go on in the same old dull road, wherein a great part of Children's time is lost in a tiresome heaping up a Pack of dry and unprofitable, or pernicious Notions (for surely little xxxi better can be said of a

all other men, according to my wont, to their own discretion and liberty, to use or refuse it, as they please. So soon then as a child can read English perfectly, and is brought to us to school to learn Latin, I would have him together with his Accidence, to be provided of this Book, in which he may at least once a day (beside his Accidence) be thus exercised.

I. Let him look over the pictures with their general titles and inscriptions, till he be able to turn readily to any one of them, and to tell its name either in English or Latin. By this means he shall xxiii have the method of the Book in his head; and be easily furnished with the knowledge of most things; and instructed how to call them, when at any time he meeteth with them elsewhere, in their real forms.

II. Let him read the description at large: First in English, and afterward in Latin, till he can readily read, and distinctly pronounce the words in both Languages, ever minding how they are spelled. And withal, let him take notice of the figures inserted, and to what part of the picture they direct by their like till he be well able to find out every particular thing of himself, and to name it on a sudden, either in English or Latin. Thus he shall not only gain the most primitive words, but be understandingly grounded in Orthography, which is a thing too generally neglected by us; partly because our English schools think that children should learn it at the Latin, and our Latin schools suppose they have already learn'd it at the English; partly, because our common Grammar is too much defective in this part, and scholars so little exercised therein, that they pass from schools to the Universities and return from thence (some of them) more unable to write true English, than either Latin or Greek. Not to speak of our ordinary Tradesmen, many of whom write such false English, that none but themselves can interpret what they scribble in their bills and shop-books.

III. Then let him get the Titles and Descriptions by heart, which he will more easily do, by reason of these impressions which the viewing of the pictures hath already made in his memory. And now let him also learn, 1. To construe, or give the words one by xxiv one, as they answer one another in Latin and English. 2. To Parse, according to the rules, (which I presume by this time) he hath learn'd in the first part of his Accidence; where I would have him tell what part of Speech any word is, and then what accidents belong to it; but especially to decline the nouns and conjugate the verbs according to the Examples in his Rudiments; and this doing will enable him to know the end and use of his Accidence. As for the Rules of Genders of Nouns, and the Præter-perfect-tenses and Supines of Verbs, and those of Concordance and Construction in the latter part of the Accidence, I would not have a child much troubled with them, till by the help of this Book he can perfectly practise so much of Etymology, as concerns the first part of his Accidence only. For that, and this book together, being thoroughly learn'd by at least thrice going them over, will much prepare children to go chearfully forward in their Grammar and School-Authors, especially, if whilst they are employed herein, they be taught also to write a fair and legible hand.

There is one thing to be given notice of, which I wish could have been remedied in this Translation; that the Book being writ in high-Dutch doth express many things in reference to that Country and Speech, which cannot without alteration of some Pictures as well as words be expressed in ours: for the Symbolical Alphabet is fitted for German children rather than for ours. And whereas the words of that Language go orderly one for one with the Latin, our English propriety of Speech will not admit the like. Therefore it will behove those Masters that intend xxv to make use of this Book, to construe it verbatim to their young Scholars, who will quickly learn to do it of themselves, after they be once acquainted with the first words of Nouns, and Verbs, and their manner of variation.

Such a work as this, I observe to have been formerly much desired by some experienced Teachers, and I my self had some years since (lived) begun the most agreeable to dren, who are mo tures from their them the knowle they seem to rep Children are as y easily conveyed t But for as much done, though in completely as it w joyce in the use o own undertakings because any goo being the more c herein imitated a to impart to othe well liked. You th of little Children, their thoughts and with bare Gramm to them are harsh retaining; because signifie nothing, notion of a gene know not what comprehend parti the like subsidiar with some know words wherewith then their Rules o ter understood an mind. Else how sh what a Rule mean ther knoweth wha porteth, nor what which is signifie native Language, thereby to under Rules consisting o livered (as I may presuming first th words to be alread ing which they are enlarge upon this very Basis of our into the way of Ch little and little of that so we may ap reach: But I leave of to your own da rience got thereby

And I pray God er of all wisdom,

) advertisement to
e the first *tasks of*
ttle and single, we
ook of training one
imself, with noth-
t is, with the chief
r with the grounds
nd the whole lan-
our understanding
re perfect descrip-
 fuller knowledge
learer light of the
i sought after (as
y are to be found
here will now be
is our *little Ency-*
oject to the senses.
 to be said touch-
use of this book.
 children into their
nselves withal as
 sight of the pic-
em as familiar to
, and that even at
out to school.
be examined ever
now in the school)
at thing is, and is
 may see nothing
how to name, and
othing which they
gs named them be
ne Picture, but al-
example, the parts
books, the house,
ffered also to im-
and, if they will,
 encouraged, that
rst, thus to quick-
owards the things;
proportion of the
ther; and lastly to
ess of the hand,
y things.
 mentioned, can-
 eye, it will be to
er them by them-
as colours, relish-
 here be pictured
ch reason it were
ngs rare and not
t home, xix might
great school, that

they may be shewed also, as often as any words are to be made of them, to the scholars.

Thus at last this school would indeed become a school of things obvious to the senses, and an entrance to the school intellectual. But enough: Let us come to the thing it self.

xx

The Translator, to all judicious and industrious School-Masters.

Gentlemen.

There are a few of you (I think) but have seen, and with great willingness made use of (or at least perused,) many of the Books of this well-deserving Author Mr. John Comenius, which for their profitableness to the speedy attainment of a language, have been translated in several countries, out of Latin into their own native tongue.

Now the general verdict (after trial made) that hath passed, touching those formerly extant, is this, that they are indeed of singular use, and very advantageous to those of more discretion, (especially to such as already have a smattering of Latin) to help their memories to retain what they have scatteringly gotten here and there, to furnish them with many words, which (perhaps) they had not formerly read, or so well observed; but to young children (whom we have chiefly to instruct) as those that are ignorant altogether of things and words, and prove rather a meer toil and burthen, than a delight and furtherance.

For to pack up many words in memory, of things not conceived in the mind, is to fill the head with empty imaginations, and to make the learner more xxi to admire the multitude and variety (and thereby, to become discouraged,) than to care to treasure them up, in hopes to gain more knowledge of what they mean.

He hath therefore in some of his latter works seemed to move retrograde, and striven to come nearer the reach of tender wits: and in this present Book, he hath, according to my judgment, descended to the very bottom of what is to be taught, and proceeded (as nature it self doth) in an orderly way; first to exercise the senses well, by representing their objects to them, and then to fasten upon the intellect by impressing the first notions of things upon it, and linking them on to another by a rational discourse. Whereas indeed, we, generally missing this way, do teach children as we do parrots, to speak they know not what, nay which is worse, we, taking the way of teaching little ones by Grammar only at the first, do puzzle their imaginations with abstractive terms and secondary intentions, which till they be somewhat acquainted with things, and the words belonging to them, in the language which they learn, they cannot apprehend what they mean. And this I guess to be the reason, why many great persons do resolve sometimes not to put a child to school till he be at least eleven or twelve years of age, presuming that he having then taken notice of most things, will sooner get the knowledge of the words which are applyed to them in any language. But the gross misdemeanor of such children for the most part, have taught many parents to be hasty enough to send their own to school, if not that they may learn, yet (at least) that they might be kept out xxii of harm's way; and yet if they do not profit for the time they have been at school, (no respect at all being had for their years) the Master shall be sure enough to bear the blame.

So that a School-master had need to bend his wits to come within the compass of a child's capacity of six or seven years of age (seeing we have now such commonly brought to our Grammar-schools to learn the Latin Tongue) and to make that they may learn with as much delight and willingness, as himself would teach with dexterity and ease. And at present I know no better help to forward his young scholars than this little Book, which was for this purpose contrived by the Author in the German and Latin Tongues.

What profitable use may be had thereof, respecting chiefly that his own country and language, he himself hath told you in his preface; but what use we may here make of it in our Grammar-schools, as it is now translated into English, I shall partly declare; leaving

ed to the senses, for fear they may not be received. I say, and say it again aloud, that this last is the foundation of all the rest: because we can neither act nor speak wisely, unless we first rightly understand all the things which are xiv to be done, and whereof we are to speak. Now there is nothing in the understanding, which was not before in the sense. And therefore to exercise the senses well about the right perceiving the differences of things, will be to lay the grounds for all wisdom, and all wise discourse, and all discreet actions in ones course of life. Which, because it is commonly neglected in schools, and the things which are to be learned are offered to scholars, without being understood or being rightly presented to the senses, it cometh to pass, that the work of teaching and learning goeth heavily onward, and affordeth little benefit.

See here then a new help for schools, A Picture and Nomenclature of all the chief things in the world, and of men's actions in their way of living: Which, that you, good Masters, may not be loath to run over with your scholars, I will tell you, in short, what good you may expect from it.

It is *a little Book*, as you see, of no great bulk, yet a brief of the whole world, and a whole language: full of Pictures, Nomenclatures, and Descriptions of things.

I. *The Pictures* are the representation of all visible things, (to which also things invisible are reduced after their fashion) of the whole world. And that in that very order of things, in which they are described in the *Janua Latinæ Linguæ*; and with that fulness, that nothing very necessary or of great concernment is omitted.

II. *The Nomenclatures* are the Inscriptions, or Titles set every one over their own Pictures, expressing the whole thing by its own general term.
xv
III. *The Descriptions* are the explications of the parts of the Picture, so expressed by their own proper terms, as that same figure which is added to every piece of the picture, and the term of it, always sheweth what things belongeth one to another.

Which such Book, and in such a dress may (I hope) serve,

I. To entice witty children to it, that they may not conceit a torment to be in the school, but dainty fare. For it is apparent, that children (even from their infancy almost) are delighted with Pictures, and willingly please their eyes with these lights: And it will be very well worth the pains to have once brought it to pass, that scare-crows may be taken away out of Wisdom's Gardens.

II. This same little Book will serve to stir up the Attention, which is to be fastened upon things, and even to be sharpened more and more: which is also a great matter. For the Senses (being the main guides of childhood, because therein the mind doth not as yet raise up itself to an abstracted contemplation of things) evermore seek their own objects, and if they be away, they grow dull, and wry themselves hither and thither out of a weariness of themselves: but when their objects are present, they grow merry, wax lively, and willingly suffer themselves to be fastened upon them, till the thing be sufficiently discerned. This Book then will do a good piece of service in taking (especially flickering) wits, and preparing them for deeper studies.

III. Whence a third good will follow; that children being won hereunto, and drawn over with this xvi way of heeding, may be furnished with the knowledge of the prime things that are in the world, by sport and merry pastime. In a word, this Book will serve for the more pleasing using of the *Vestibulum* and *Janua Linguarum*, for which end it was even at the first chiefly intended. Yet if it like any, that it be bound up in their native tongues also, it promiseth three good thing of itself.

I. First it will afford a device for learning to read more easily than hitherto, especially having a symbolical alphabet set before it, to wit, the characters of the several letters, with the image of that creature, whose voice that letter goeth about to imitate, pictur'd by it. For the young *Abc* scholar will easily remember the force by the very looking till the imagination by use, can readily then having looked *chief syllables* also thought necessary book) he may pro of the Pictures, and over 'em. Where a upon the thing pic name of the thing, title of the picture thus the whole boo the bare titles of cannot but be lear which thing is to b ing any ordinary most troublesome may wholly be ave For the often readi those larger descri which are set after able perfectly to b ing.
xvii
II. The same book lish, in English Sc the perfect learnin lish tongue, and th because by the afo things, the words whole language ar their own places. Grammar might b clearly resolving th derstood in o ts p clining of the seve ing those that are certain rules.

III. Thence a that that very Eng serve for the mor learning of the Lat see in this Edition ing so translated, word answereth against it, and the the same, only in clad in a double might be also so advertisements ad ing those things of the Latin tong English. For whe

things afterwards
ames of Pestalozzi
be safely assumed
at are now in prac-
ot unknown to ear-
's Systems of Edu-
, p. 13.
t on the method of
ve shall see it is re-
ness, and we shall
much wisdom can
 of schoolmasters
ifty years, and that
ped to avail them-
s. — Browning's
History of Educa-
2, New York edi-

' the first practical
uitive method, had
uccess, and has
r the innumerable
ich for three cen-
 the schools. —
 of Pedagogy ,
Boston, 1886, p.

Patak four years,
ized by surprising
ng this short peri-
ss than fifteen dif-
 them his "World
ctus), the most fa-
gs. ix It admirably
 that words and
ned together . . .
ted" had an enor-
d remained for a
pular text-book in
History of Educa-
06.

t qu'un <u>équivalent</u>
on; si, ensuite, le
t fort <u>défectueux</u>,
la science de nos
fort exagéré pour
eption de l'enfant
es modernes, trop
nes qui paraissent
tus était pourtant,
oeuvre très origi-
e, qui fit faire un
dagogie et servit
'école utile et de
mbrables livres

d'images, souvent pires. —<u>Histoire</u> d'Éducation, Frederick Dittes , Redolfi's French translation, Paris, 1880, p. 178.

Here Comenius wrote, among others, his second celebrated work the "Orbis Pictus." He was not, however, able to finish it in Hungary for want of a skilful engraver on copper. For such a one he carried it to Michael Endter, the bookseller at Nuremberg, but the engraving delayed the publication of the book for three years more. In 1657 Comenius expressed the hope that it would appear during the next autumn. With what great approbation the work was received at its first appearance, is shown by the fact that within two years, in 1659, Endter had published a second enlarged edition. — Karl Von x Raumer, translated in Barnard's Journal of Education, v. 260.

The "Janua" had an enormous sale, and was published in many languages, but the editions and sale of the "Orbis Pictus" far exceeded those of the "Janua," and, indeed, for some time it was the most popular text-book in Europe, and deservedly so. — Laurie's John Amos Comenius , Boston edition, p. 185.
[xi]

> JOH. AMOS COMENII
> **Orbis Sensualium Pictus:**
> HOC EST
> Omnium principalium in Mundo Rerum, & in Vita Actionum,
> PICTURA & NOMENCLATURA.
>
> JOH. AMOS COMENIUS's
> **VISIBLE WORLD:**
> OR, A
> Nomenclature, and Pictures
> OF ALL THE
> CHIEF THINGS that are in the WORLD, and of MENS EMPLOYMENTS therein;
> In above 150 COPPER CUTS.
> WRITTEN
> By the Author in Latin and High Dutch, being one of his last ESSAYS; and the most suitable to Childrens Capacity of any he hath hitherto made.
> Translated into English
> By CHARLES HOOLE, M. A.
> For the Use of Young Latin Scholars.
> The ELEVENTH EDITION Corrected, and the English made to answer Word for Word to the Latin.
> *Nihil est in intellectu, quod non prius fuit in sensu.* Arist.
> London; Printed for, and sold by *John* and *Benj. Sprint*, at the *Bell* in *Little Britain*, 1728.

Text
[xii]

Gen. ii. 19, 20.

The Lord God brought unto *Adam* every Beast of the Field, and every Fowl of the Air, to see what he would call them. And *Adam* gave Names to all Cattle, and to the Fowl of the Air, and to every Beast of the Field.

Gen. ii. 19, 20.

Adduxit Dominus Deus ad Adam cuncta Animantia Terræ, & universa volatilia Cœli, ut videret quomodo vocaret illa. Appellavitque Adam Nominibus suis cuncta Animantia, & universa volatilia Cœli, & omnes Bestias Agri.

I. A. Comenii opera Didactica par. 1. p. 6, Amst. 1657. fol.

Didacticæ nostræ prora & puppis esto: Investigare, & invenire modum, quo Docentes minus doceant, Discentes vero plus discant: Scholæ minus habeant Strepitus, nauseæ, vani laboris; plus autem otii, deliciarum, solidique profectus: Respublica Christiana minus tenebrarum confusionis dissidiorum; plus lucis, ordinis, pacis & tranquilitatis.
xiii

The Author's Preface to the Reader.

*I*nstruction is the means to expel *Rudeness*, with which young wits ought to be well furnished in Schools: But so, as that the teaching be 1. *True*, 2. *Full*, 3. *Clear*, and 4. *Solid*.

1. It will be *true*, if nothing be taught but such as is beneficial to ones life; lest there be a cause of complaining afterwards. We know not necessary things, because we have not learned things necessary.

2. It will be *full*, if the mind be polished for wisdom, the tongue for eloquence, and the hands for a neat way of living. This will be that *grace* of one's life, *to be wise, to act, to speak*.

3, 4. It will be *clear*, and by that, firm and *solid*, if whatever is taught and learned, be not obscure, or confused, but apparent, distinct, and articulate, as the fingers on the hands.

The ground of this business, is, that sensual objects may be rightly present-

inal cut of the Soul, (No. 43, as here given,) a picture of an eye, and in a table the figures I. I. II. I I. II., and adds that it is difficult to recognize in this an expressive psychological symbol, and to explain it. In an edition I have, published in Vienna in 1779, this cut is omitted altogether, and indeed there are but 82 in place of the 157 found in earlier editions, the following, as numbered in this edition, being omitted:

1, the alphabet, 2, 36, 43, 45, 66, 68, 75, 76, 78–80, 87, 88, 92–122, 124, 126, 128, 130–141.

iv

On the other hand, the Vienna edition contains a curious additional cut. It gives No. 4, the Heaven, practically as in this edition, but puts another cut under it in which the earth is revolving about the sun; and after the statement of Comenius, "*Coelum rotatur, et ambit terram, in medio stantem*" interpolates: "*prout veteres crediderunt, recentiores enim defendunt motum terrae circa solem*" [as the ancients used to think; for later authorities hold that the motion of the earth is about the sun.]

Two specimen pages from another edition are inserted in Payne's Compayré's History of Education (between pp. 126, 127). The cut is the representative of No. 103 in this edition, but those who compare them will see not only how much coarser is the execution of the wood-cut Prof. Payne has copied, but what liberties have been taken with the design. The only change in the Latin text, however, is from *Designat Figuras rerum* in the original, to *Figuram rerum designat*.

In this edition the cuts are unusually clear copies of the copper-plates of the first edition of 1658, from which we have also taken the Latin text. The text for the English translation is from the English edition of 1727, in which for the first time the English words were so arranged as to stand opposite their Latin equivalents.

The cuts have been reproduced with great care by the photographic process. I thought best not to permit them to be retouched, preferring occasional indistinctness to modern tampering with the originals that would make them less authentic.

v

The English text is unchanged from that of the 1727 edition, except in rare instances where substitutions have been made for single words not now permissible. The typography suggests rather than imitates the quaintness of the original, and the paper was carefully selected to produce so far as practicable the impression of the old hand-presses.

In short my aim has been to put within the reach of teachers at a moderate price a satisfactory reproduction of this important book; and if the sale of the *Orbis Pictus* seems to warrant it, I hope subsequently to print as a companion volume the *Vestibulum* and *Janua* of the same author, of which I have choice copies.

C. W. Bardeen.
Syracuse, Sept. 28, 1887.

vi

Comments upon the Orbis Pictus.

During four years he here prosecuted his efforts in behalf of education with commendable success, and wrote, among other works, his celebrated Orbis Pictus, which has passed through a great many editions, and survived a multitude of imitations. — Smith's History of Education, N.Y., 1842, p. 129.

The most eminent educator of the seventeenth century, however, was John Amos Comenius . . . . . . His Orbis Sensualium Pictus, published in 1657, enjoyed a still higher renown. The text was much the same with the Janua, being intended as a kind of elementary encyclopædia; but *it differed from all previous text-books*, in being illustrated with pictures, on copper and wood, of the various topics discussed in it. This book was universally popular. In those portions of Germany where the schools had been broken up by the "Thirty years' war," mothers taught their children from its pages. Corrected and amended by later editors, it continued for nearly two hundred years, to be a text-book of the German schools. — History and Progress of Education, by Philobiblius, N.Y., 1860, p. 210.

The "Janua" w[as] had but a short-l[ived] teachers, and a st[...] ers, if Comenius h[...] vii principle of ap[...] and called in the the "Orbis Pictus," a favorite with [...] maintained its gro[...] for more than a ce[...] I cannot give a s[...] ebrated book wit[...] The artist, of cour[...] technical skill wh[...] ly displayed even cations, but this re[...] none the less ente[...] of the life and m[...] teenth century, th[...] torical interest, w[...] cure for it anothe[...] Quick's Education Syracuse edition, [...]

But the princip[...] insisted is that th[...] and things must [...] hand. When we time is spent over waste of energy preparation, how [...] foundation that th[...] building upon it, [...] it is in the accepta[...] of this principle th[...] education will in t[...] one who attempts reform will find t[...] are contained in t[...] nius. — Encyclop[...] edition, vii. 674.

The first editi[...] book was publis[...] 1657; soon after a[...] into English by C[...] English edition a[...] this was reprinted This was the first book, and was th[...] now passes unde[...] lessons." — Shor[...], W. H. Payne, S[...]

Of these, the "[...] were translated in[...] some of the Orien[...] ident that these p[...]

1887.

Copyright, 1887, by C. W. Bardeen .
ii

It may not be generally known that Comenius was once solicited to become President of Harvard College. The following is a quotation from Vol. II, p. 14, of Cotton Mather's Magnalia :

"That brave old man, Johannes Amos Commenius, the fame of whose worth has been TRUMPETTED as far as more than three languages (whereof everyone is indebted unto his Janua) could carry it, was indeed agreed withal, by one Mr. Winthrop in his travels through the LOW COUNTRIES , to come over to New England, and illuminate their Colledge and COUNTRY , in the quality of a President, which was now become vacant. But the solicitations of the Swedish Ambassador diverting him another way, that incomparable Moravian became not an American."

This was on the resignation of President Dunster, in 1654— Note of Prof. Payne, Compayre's History of Education, Boston , 1886, p. 125.
iii

Editor's Preface.

When it is remembered that this work is not only an educational classic of prime importance, but that it was the first picture-book ever made for children and was for a century the most popular text-book in Europe, and yet has been for many years unattainable on account of its rarity, the wonder is, not that it is reproduced now but that it has not been reproduced before. But the difficulty has been to find a satisfactory copy. Many as have been the editions, few copies have been preserved. It was a book children were fond of and wore out in turning the leaves over and over to see the pictures. Then as the old copper-plates became indistinct they were replaced by wood-engravings, of coarse execution, and often of changed treatment. Von Raumer complains that the edition of 1755 substitutes for the orig-

If any of these characters do not display properly—in particular, if the diacritic does not appear directly above the letter—or if the apostrophes and quotation marks in this paragraph appear as garbage, you may have an incompatible browser or unavailable fonts. First, make sure that the browser's "character set" or "file encoding" is set to Unicode (UTF-8). You may also need to change your browser's default font.

The two sections numbered CIV use astrological symbols. Most are accompanied by a definition, so the meaning will be plain even if your browser cannot display them. When a symbol is used in place of a word, its meaning is shown in a popup: ☉ .

Typographical errors are shown in the text with <u>mouse-hover popups</u>. In the *Orbis Pictus* text, apparent errors in punctuation and typography (such as Italic type where Roman is expected) were unchanged except in chapter headers, where readers may need the exact format for text searches. Uncorrected errors are <u>noted with popups</u>. Note that "Dutch" generally means "German".

Line breaks are approximately but not exactly the same as in the original.

THE

ORBIS PICTUS

OF

John Amos Comenius.

This work is, indeed, the first children's picture book.
— **Encyclopædia Britannica, 9th Edition , vi. 182.**

SYRACUSE, N. Y.:
C. W. BARDEEN, PUBLISHER,